ZAFER ŞENOCAK

Atlas of a Tropical Germany

Essays on Politics and Culture,
1990–1998

TRANSLATED AND EDITED BY

LESLIE A. ADELSON

University of Nebraska Press

Lincoln and London

Publication of this book was assisted by a grant from the National Endowment for the Arts. Sources of foreign-language originals appear on pages vii–ix, which constitute an extension of the copyright page. Copyright © 2000 by the University of Nebraska Press. All rights reserved. ⊗ Manufactured in the United States of America

Library of Congress Cataloging-in-Publication Data
Şenocak, Zafer, 1961–
Atlas of a tropical Germany: essays on politics and culture, 1900–1998 / Zafer Şenocak ; translated and edited by Leslie A. Adelson. p. cm. – (Texts and contexts)
Selected chiefly from Atlas des tropischen Deutschland (published in 1992) and War Hitler Araber? (Published in 1994). Includes bibliographical references and index.
ISBN 0-8032-9275-9 (pbk.: alkaline paper) 1. Germany – Geography. 2. Germany – Ethnic relations. 3. Political culture – Germany. 4. Multiculturalism – Germany.
I. Adelson, Leslie A. II. Şenocak, Zafer, 1961– Atlas des tropischen Deutschland. III. Şenocak, Zafer, 1961– War Hitler Araber? IV. Title. V. Texts and contexts (Unnumbered) DD21.3.S46 2000 943.087′9–dc21 00-020992

Contents

Contents

Sources

Zafer Şenocak holds the rights to all his essays and interviews in any language that have been selected for inclusion in this *Atlas of a Tropical Germany: Essays on Politics and Culture, 1990–1998*. They appear in English translation here with the express permission of the author. His preface, "To My Readers in the United States," was written specifically for this publication. Two anthologies of the author's essays published previously contain the original German versions of several essays that have been included here. This applies to *Atlas des tropischen Deutschland: Essays* (Berlin: Babel, 1992), which includes "Deutschland—Heimat für Türken?" ["Germany—Home for Turks?"], written together with Bülent Tulay (9–19); "Die Insel: Ein Reisebericht" ["The Island: A Travelogue"] (50–55); "Was hat Waldsterben mit multikultureller Gesellschaft zu tun?" ["What Does the Forest Dying Have to Do with Multiculturalism?"] (39–44); "Tradition und Tabu" ["Tradition and Taboo"] (94–96); and "Dialog über die dritte Sprache" ["Dialogue about the Third Language"] (85–90). It applies as well to *War Hitler Araber? IrreFührungen an den Rand Europas, Essays* (Berlin: Babel, 1994), which includes "War Adolf Hitler Araber? Über die Sprache der Experten, wenn sie vor weissen Flecken stehen" ["Was Adolf Hitler an Arab? On the Language of Experts When Confronted with Blank Spots"] (65–67); " 'Orient' und 'Okzident': am Scheideweg?" [" 'Orient' and 'Occident': At the Crossroads?"] (68–74); "Der Dichter und die Deserteure: Rushdie und seine *Satanischen Verse* zwischen den Fronten" ["The Poet and the Deserters: Salman Rushdie between the Fronts"] (21–28); and "Das Unbehagen am Kulturbegriff" ["The Concept of Culture and Its Discontents"] (59–64). The essay "Tradition und Tabu" was first translated into English by Judith Orban, then Programme Coordinator for the Goethe-Institut Toronto, in conjunction with a conference sponsored by that organization in Fall 1993 on "Identity in a Foreign Place," at which the author was a featured speaker. Judith Orban's translation was subsequently published as "Tradition and Taboo" in the Canadian literary journal *Descant* 83 [vol. 24, no. 4] (winter 1993–94): 147–48. Only minor changes have been made in that translation in order to bring it into line with editorial preferences guiding the present volume overall. Judith Orban, the Goethe-Institut Toronto, and the *Descant* Arts and Letters Foundation have graciously consented to this use of Judith Orban's original translation.

The remaining essays are drawn from a variety of sources, and a few are published here for the first time. "Thoughts on May 8, 1995" has been translated from "Gedanken zum 8. Mai 1995," in *Vom Vergessen, vom Gedenken*, edited by Brigitte Sauzay, Heinz Ludwig Arnold, and Rudolf von Thadden (Göttingen: Wallstein, 1995) 91–93. "Between Orient and Occident" first appeared as "Zwischen Orient und Okzident," *Die Zeit* no. 22 (May 26, 1995): 55. The English translation of "Germany Is More a Language Than a Land" is based on an unpublished German translation of an interview conducted with the author in Turkish by Halil Gökhan. Mine Dal and Karin Yeşilada, who jointly prepared the German translation, have kindly agreed to its use in this regard. The Turkish original appeared in an Istanbul journal as "Almanya Bir Ülke Olmaktan Çok Bir Dildir," *Kitaplık* 12 (October–December 1994): 24. "May One Compare Turks and Jews, Mr. Şenocak?" is a translation of an interview conducted with the author in German by Karin Yeşilada for a daily newspaper in Berlin; "Darf man Türken und Juden vergleichen, Herr Şenocak?" was published in the *Tagesspiegel* (April 13–14, 1995): 26. The multilingual literary journal *Sirene* [Munich] 9.15/16 (March 1996) includes "Jenseits der Landessprache" (171–73), which appears here as "Beyond the Language of the Land." The same issue of *Sirene* includes as well "'. . . der Mensch, / der's mit anhört, . . .'" (166–70), which represents an earlier version of the revised essay that appears here with the title "Paul Celan." A somewhat different German version of "The One and the Other Child" was published as part of the author's novel, *Gefährliche Verwandtschaft* (Berlin: Babel, 1998), 98–99. Earlier versions of "Territories" and "Which Myth Writes Me?" were presented as lectures for university audiences in the United States. They are published in this volume for the first time. The essay that is included here as "War and Peace in Modernity: Reflections on the German-Turkish Future (1994/1998)" has had more than one predecessor, but none that corresponds exactly to the revised German manuscript that provided the foundation for this translation. An early German version appeared as "Krieg und Frieden in Deutschland—Gedanken über die deutsch-türkische Zukunft" in *Anderssein, ein Menschenrecht: Über die Vereinbarkeit universaler Normen mit kultureller und ethnischer Vielfalt*, edited by Hilmar Hoffmann and Dieter Kramer (Weinheim: Beltz Athenäum, 1995), 115–23. Martin Chalmers prepared the published English translation of a modified version of that essay, which is available in print only as "War and Peace in Modernity: Reflections on the German-Turkish Future (1994)," *Cultural Studies* 10.2 (May 1996): 255–69, with a brief critical introduction by Kevin Robins. For the purposes of the present *Atlas of a Tropical Germany*, and in light of intervening political developments, the author modified and expanded his essay again in 1998. This most recent version appears here as "War and Peace in Modernity: Reflections on the German-Turkish Future (1994/1998)," as translated by Martin Chalmers and Leslie A. Adelson. This translation includes minor emendations and substantive additions to the essay in *Cultural Studies*, a publication of Routledge Journals, but it nonetheless relies significantly on the Chalmers translation of 1996. Martin Chalmers has generously granted permission to use his translation in this manner, as has Routledge Journals, a subsidiary of Taylor & Francis Ltd., 11 New Fetter Lane, London EC4P 4EE, England. With the exception of "War and Peace in Modernity" and "Tradition and Taboo," all translations into English have been prepared by Leslie A. Adelson, who has also edited the entire volume.

Leslie A. Adelson

Coordinates of Orientation

AN INTRODUCTION

The map of Germany changed rather dramatically on October 3, 1990, when the two postwar German states of the Federal Republic of Germany (West) and the German Democratic Republic (East) were united as the newly configured Federal Republic of Germany.[1] The geographical transformation, which was simply additive, also entailed a political transition, one for which no simple mathematical equation can be found. When does 1+1 = 1? Does 1+1 (necessarily and always) = 2? How can 1+1 be made or encouraged to equal a politically unified Germany? The initial euphoria sparked by the fall of the Berlin Wall soon gave way to the pragmatic difficulties and social uncertainties of a national unification that was not merely ideological and constitutional but also lived and contested.[2] While many West Germans bristled at bearing the financial brunt of unification (but otherwise had few adjustments to make in their daily routines and thinking habits), many East Germans suddenly faced a profound loss of orientation in an unfamiliar labor market, a hostile political climate, and a Germany to which they now belonged but barely knew.[3] One of West Germany's most vocal public intellectuals once predicted in 1982 that it would ultimately prove far more difficult to undo "the wall in the head" than the real one, and the first decade of postwar unification would seem to confirm the accuracy of this prediction, for East and West alike.[4]

At the same time, the results of the federal elections in September 1998 suggest that Westerners and Easterners are working together, and perhaps not only in parliament, to articulate a new orientation for a unified Germany beyond the Cold War, one that looks even more to a European future than to a troubled German past.[5] Commonly hailed as the architect of unification, the conservative Helmut

Kohl was until recently a surprisingly and successfully tenacious politician, whose sixteen years of service as federal chancellor exceeded that of any other West German statesman of the postwar era. When the parties and policies that he represented were defeated in fall 1998 by a coalition of Social Democrats and Greens, the victory of these opposition parties signaled more than a political or even a generational change in leadership.[6] Beyond this, one might say that the 1998 elections marked the end of the postwar period in ways that the formal unification could not possibly have accomplished overnight.

Every epoch shapes and ponders the meaning of its present, between the past that inspires or haunts it and the future that it strives to create.[7] This was perhaps especially true of the first Federal Republic of Germany (1949–90), a democratic state founded in the shadow of the Third Reich, at the epicenter of the Cold War, and en route to the unified Germany that would supersede it.[8] Now that Germany's East and West have been united and the Cold War has ended, the emergent Federal Republic turns to tasks that are necessarily new, the challenge of European integration foremost among them.[9] This does not mean that the Nazi past ceases to be a topic of concern or controversy, as recent and ongoing debates about the proposed National Monument to the Murdered Jews of Europe or about Martin Walser's provocative rejection of Auschwitz as a "moral cudgel" attest.[10] What it does clearly mean is that the 1990s have been a remarkable decade of epochal transitions for Germany and for Europe. Many of these transitions have yet to be fully understood, in part because we do not yet know the shape of the future that lies just ahead.

Where are Germany's resident Turks to be located on this map? Do they enter into a relationship with the German past when they enter German territory, or when they build lives over generations there? What relationships do and will they have to the German future? Can the post-Wall encounter between East and West be understood only as a "German-German" dialogue? These, I suggest, are important questions. Spanning the pivotal decade of the 1990s, the essays gathered here prompt us to entertain them more critically and more profoundly than has been done to date. To the extent that related questions about the largest minority population in Germany today have been raised or intimated at all, the answers proffered have tended to be the obvious ones, perhaps too obvious. They might be summed up in terms of two primary categories: right-wing xenophobia and exclusionary citizenship. Especially in the wake of unification, both issues have been repeatedly invoked—rightly or wrongly—as a kind of litmus test for the character and values of the newly unified German state. How democratic, civilized, and European is it?[11] Some broad strokes will have to suffice here to clarify how these invocations operate.

Although there are different opinions as to the political status of xenophobic violence in the 1990s (spurred by right-wing fringe organizations or perpetrated by socially disenfranchised individuals?), statistics clearly indicate that the early years of unification were marred by a sharp increase in physical attacks on foreigners, those who really were foreigners or those who merely (and allegedly) "looked like" foreigners. As one expert on German social movements has noted, the vast majority of both East and West Germans disapproved of xenophobic violence prior to unification.[12] While most Germans in unified Germany continued to deplore such violence, they had all the more occasion to do so publicly when some horrific incidents shocked people into an awareness that racism and xenophobia were taking a markedly violent turn.[13] "The turning-point for the Federal Republic with regard to open displays of anti-foreigner sentiment was not 1992 but 1991, the year during which the number of attacks against foreigners increased ten-fold on German soil."[14] The reference to 1992 is crucial for our purposes, because in late November of that year, in the town of Mölln, one elderly Turkish woman and two Turkish children were killed (and several others injured) in an arson attack on their home. These murders were followed six months later, in May 1993, by another lethal fire-bombing of a private residence, this time in Solingen, where five Turkish women and children lost their lives and nine other people were hurt. The names of these West German towns—Mölln and Solingen—have served ever since as a kind of electrifying emblem for real and potential dangers, for political instabilities and social anxieties that struck an alarming note in an otherwise celebratory, optimistic, and early phase of unification. Even though the criminals were apprehended and sentenced to prison, and even though thousands of Germans expressed their grief and solidarity with the Turkish minority by participating in long candlelight processions throughout the country, the symbolic significance of Mölln and Solingen was and remains especially acute for the younger generations of Turks, many of whom have grown up in Germany and consider it their home, with or without citizenship.[15] For one defiant young woman interviewed in 1998, the deadly arson attacks signal, literally, a turning point in the telling of time, a dividing line: "for we say here: the time before the fire and time after it."[16]

For non-Turkish Germans, too, Mölln and Solingen have a symbolic ring, at once smoldering and chilling, a ring they share with other place-names associated with violence against "outsiders."[17] Hoyerswerda, a former coal-mining town in the East German state of Saxony, drew international attention in September 1991 when a large group of rabble-rousers attacked a dormitory for foreign laborers, including Yugoslavs, Mozambicans, and Turks. Applause from a sizable crowd of onlookers fueled the public outcry that news of this incident subsequently provoked. Before another year had passed, a former ship-building center on the Baltic Sea had become another flash point for antiforeigner violence. In August 1992 two adjacent residences—temporary homes to Romanian asylum seekers and Vietnamese laborers—were set ablaze with Molotov cocktails. The attendant rioting by the attackers in Rostock-Lichtenhagen lasted a week.[18] The first few years of unification thus saw a dramatic surge in violent hostilities directed against a wide range of permanent residents, asylum seekers, "foreign-looking" citizens, and migrant workers.[19] Despite the diversity among the victims of these attacks, the Turks in Germany stand out both symbolically and statistically. Because they number approximately two million, they account collectively for roughly 28 percent of the over 7 million foreigners residing in unified Germany (among a total population of more than 82 million).[20] German xenophobia and the Turkish presence are linked in the popular imagination, such that many people find it difficult to relate to one without simultaneously expressing some kind of relationship to the other. In this associative vein, any news about Turks in Germany tends to trigger some assessment of how well the unified nation counters xenophobic sentiments and strengthens its democratic convictions. Public concern for Turkish vulnerabilities, however, does not necessarily entail substantive familiarity or sustained interaction with Turkish lives in the Federal Republic. As the essays made available here critically contend, this simultaneous attention to Turks and ignorance of their culture have both political and social repercussions for the new Federal Republic, its present as well as its possible future. (On the subject of "their culture," I provide additional remarks below.)

These essays were intended (and may still be understood) as pressing interventions in a crucial transitional period of German life, culture, and politics beyond the Cold War and at the end of the millennium, but also at the dawn of something new. If the decade in which they were written opened, among other things, with brutal attacks on Turks and other "outsiders," it closed with consideration of a radical liberalization of Germany's citizenship law. This prospect, which had the potential to make many more political rights available generally to Turks in the Federal Republic, involves the other most commonly invoked litmus test for contemporary Germany's qualifications as a civilized Western nation.[21] Collectively, the Turks have the most compelling minority bid on membership in the German body politic, from which they have been largely excluded on the basis of a citizenship law that predated the Federal Republic and even the Third Reich and the Weimar Republic.[22] As *The Economist* put it, "When refugees have been knocking at the door in recent years, few European countries have been as open-armed as Germany, but in one respect Germany's attitude to strangers has been lamentable. Its 1913 citizenship law makes it hard for foreigners to become Germans unless they can lay claim to a German bloodline."[23] In contrast to the principle of citizenship that prevails in the United States (*jus soli*), which grants citizenship to anyone born on American territory, German citizenship has been in the first instance a matter of blood lineage (*jus sanguinis*) or familial descent. Naturalization was allowed, but only "as an exception made contingent on full cultural assimilation" and "repudiation of previous citizenship."[24] Especially after the collapse of the Soviet Union, this law made it easy for ethnic Germans from Eastern European countries (such as Poland, Russia, and Romania) to claim the rights of German citizens, even if they did not speak German and had never been to Germany.[25] For Turks, who had begun migrating to Germany in large numbers in the 1960s (without being allowed to "immigrate" in any official sense), the acquisition of German citizenship has been no easy matter at all.

Myriad ties between Turks and Germans (as well as between Turks and other Europeans) existed long before these relatively recent demographic developments. In the twentieth century alone, the Ottoman Empire and Germany were military allies in World War I, while the neutral Republic of Turkey (founded in 1923) offered a safe haven to many German Jews fleeing the Third Reich.[26] But only with the signing of a labor treaty between West Germany and Turkey in October 1961—just two months after the Berlin Wall had been raised—did the lived relationship between Turks and Germans, in Germany, begin to change in a way that would eventually have far-reaching consequences for German politics and society. This came as a surprise to virtually everyone. (And in many ways, the 1990s controversy over dual citizenship might be understood as a belated effect of this enduring surprise.) German labor shortages of the 1950s and 1960s had prompted government and industry to recruit foreign workers, on a temporary rotational basis, from several different countries, of which Turkey was only one. Italy was the first, in 1955, followed by Spain and Greece in 1960. Turkey signed on next, as did Morocco, Portugal, Tunisia, and Yugoslavia in the ensuing decade.[27] Original expectations were that individual workers would usually spend one year in Germany before returning to their home country. These were the so-called *Gastarbeiter* (guest workers), "guests" on whose behalf "no thought was given to social integration," mostly because they were not supposed to stay long enough to warrant it.[28] As both German employers and foreign laborers began to realize that longer contracts were economically (and operationally) advantageous, stays were more frequently extended. Population growth, systemic under-employment, and migration patterns in Turkey itself made oppor-tunities in Germany seem all the more attractive to a number of Turkish citizens facing an uncertain period of industrialization, dis-location, and political violence at home.[29] By the time the German government put an official halt to active recruitment of foreign la-borers in 1973 (and offered financial rewards to those who would pack up and leave their German "host" country), many Turkish workers and their families had put down roots of sorts and opted to stay.

Although the history of a sizable resident Turkish community in Germany may have begun with this decisive phase of international labor relations, the years and generations since have entailed a broad diversification of Turkish-German lives, professions, and affiliations. As the editors of *Turkish Culture in German Society Today* have re-marked, the first generation of *Gastarbeiter* is reaching retirement age while second and third generations "are beginning to write their own history, create their own place, and voice their own expectations about what it means and what it should mean for Turks to live in Germany."[30] They may be doctors, poets, educators, entrepreneurs, construction workers, filmmakers, and even members of parlia-ment.[31] Diversity among Germany's resident Turks notwithstanding, social and cultural stereotypes about Turks persist in the popular imagination and often influence public debates. And whatever differ-ences there may have been among members of this minority popula-tion in nearly forty years of German life, the law of the land made the acquisition of citizenship a matter of "discretionary naturalization" (with discretion largely in the hands of bureaucrats) rather than political entitlement.[32]

A prominent legal scholar draws our attention to the fact that

Germans are not alone among Europeans in thinking of a nation (*Nation*) or a people (*Volk*) as something different from a state (*Staat*), indeed "as an aggregate existing independent of state organization, unified by certain commonalities such as language, religion, culture, history, and descent."[33] Cultural criteria for admission to the German *Nation* are thus more nebulous than the codified prerequisites for naturalization as a citizen of the state, at least as most Americans would imagine it. Yet in the case of the long-standing German citizenship law, which was based on the Nationality Act of 1913, the expectation that successful applicants would demonstrate a subjective orientation and affective commitment (*Hinwendung*) to German values and culture brought the hazy connotations of *Nation* into the legal requirements for becoming a citizen of the state.[34] The coalition government elected in 1998 (headed by Social Democrat Gerhard Schröder) intended to change this, in part, by establishing the legal option of dual citizenship for foreign residents who would otherwise have little recourse for political involvement in the country that has become their home. Collectively, the Turkish national minority had the most to gain from such a controversial change.[35]

Why did Germany's postwar democracy wait so long to consider this course of action? (This is a question that Americans are especially likely to raise.) Gerald L. Neuman explains some of the reasons for the longevity of the 1913 citizenship law prior to unification: "The Federal Republic maintained a legal claim to continuity with the predecessor German Empire. It never recognized East Germany as a foreign state and always regarded the citizens of East Germany as sharing a common nationality with West Germans; the 1913 act provided the juridical basis for that common nationality. Since unification, that function of the 1913 act has become obsolete, and the long-delayed recodification of nationality law has become a feasible project, though a politically divisive one."[36] The extent of its divisiveness was evident, as I drafted this introduction in January 1999, in the vociferous opposition mobilized by the two main opposition parties, the Christian Democratic Union and its Bavarian coalition partner, the Christian Socialist Union. On a platform of "Yes to Integration,

No to Dual Citizenship," they conducted a nationwide signature-gathering campaign in an effort to thwart the proposal on the federal level, to appeal to the Constitutional Court (*Bundesverfassungsgericht*), and to win regional elections and support. (This attempt at something like a people's referendum was itself controversial, inasmuch as the Basic Law allows for plebiscites only in extremely restricted circumstances.) The rigorous campaign against dual citizenship succeeded in eliminating this option from parliamentary consideration in May 1999, when a less liberal but still dramatic revision of the citizenship law was finally approved.

Although the Aliens Act—which is not the same as the law governing citizenship—was liberalized somewhat in 1990 and again in 1993,[37] none of these previous reforms affecting the political status of resident Turks allowed for dual citizenship as a generalized right. There were also some features of Turkish law that had mitigated against the appeal of German citizenship if it meant the renunciation of Turkish citizenship, which it almost always did. One of these features had to do with Turkish military service, which had to be absolved (by men) before the Turkish Republic would release them legally from their obligations to their putative country of origin. (This applied even to Turks born and raised in Germany, since they were, after all, Turkish and not German citizens.) The other pertinent stipulation was that the renunciation of Turkish nationality also meant the forfeiture of the right to own or inherit property in Turkey. These two deterrents to seeking formal admission to the German body politic were eliminated by a liberalization of Turkey's own nationality law in 1995.[38] If their removal makes it easier for some Turks living in Germany to become German citizens, this does not necessarily mean that most Turks will be eager to repudiate their Turkish nationality, especially if fear of xenophobic violence in Germany plays a role.[39]

The proposal presented on January 13, 1999, by Otto Schily, the secretary of the Interior, would have made dual citizenship possible for foreigners who have lived lawfully in Germany for eight years, who can speak German and support themselves financially, and who swear allegiance to the German constitution. According to that subsequently unsuccessful proposal, children born in Germany to foreigners living in the Federal Republic would have become German citizens if at least one parent had either been born in Germany or moved there before the age of fourteen. (Additional regulations would have relaxed naturalization criteria for children over fourteen and young adults over eighteen.)[40] Effective January 1, 2000, the changes that were finally adopted allow for dual citizenship for adults only in exceptional cases. In a turn that was nonetheless historic, the approved revisions introduced a modified version of *jus soli* into German citizenship law. Any child born on German soil to at least one parent who has been in the country legally for at least eight years will automatically be entitled to German citizenship.[41]

However many Turks and other foreigners might ultimately seek German citizenship—or have children who are German citizens—because of less restrictive criteria and procedures, the debates of the 1990s tell us that the possibility of real change is warmly welcomed by some, while others feel inordinately threatened by it. (And it would be wrong to assume that all Turks are on one side of this split or that all Germans are on the other.) If the government elected in 1998 precipitated a decisive legal boiling point, the political and cultural components of the controversy were simmering for over a decade. The essays in this volume trace some of the milestones in this development, but in connecting the dots, they also draw a more complex picture of Turks and Germans than many are accustomed to seeing.

There is no question that physical safety and political rights must be secured.[42] Even if a more widely accessible path to German citizenship has been smoothed, will all pressing questions about Turkish-German relations be answered, all dilemmas resolved? Does heightened political access to citizenship for some place German Turks squarely on the map of Germany today? The allusion to cartography in Zafer Şenocak's title suggests that his essays entertain and provoke these questions, even though all the pieces presented here were written before the fall elections of 1998.[43] And I suspect that his cartographic concerns will grow more important generally (in Germany and in the international community) for the foreseeable future. This is because cultural configurations—perceptions, approximations, and conflicts—are much messier than political divisions, even as they inform (and occasionally misinform) the latter. When a CDU flyer encouraging German citizens to take an active stance against dual citizenship highlighted perceived dangers of "divided loyalties," "Islamic fundamentalism," "violent tendencies," and "unchecked immigration," was this more about politics or culture?[44] Where does one draw the line between these two realms of thought and action? Can one ever draw it absolutely? And if one agrees that these realms are somehow related but not interchangeable, what is the nature of their relationship? For the author of these essays, the urgently needed answers to such questions must be contextual, historical, and above all, imaginative. His essays are an invitation to a more profound curiosity than ready-made templates of political diatribe can allow. This is not in any simple sense curiosity about a presumed ethnic Other, but a desire to chart with greater complexity a life world and a cultural orientation shared by Germans and Turks, at a decisive turning point in their shared history.

This must seem odd to anyone whose initial point of departure is the assumption of an absolute divide between Germans and the Turks who live among them. But the notion of such a gaping chasm has itself a long history, the lines of which track a cultural topography mapped onto geographical terrain. From the Ottoman Empire's conquest of Constantinople (subsequently Istanbul) in 1453, to the military sieges of Vienna in 1529 and 1683, and beyond, the specter of an Islamic "Turkish Peril" (German: *Türkengefahr*) has haunted "the heart of Christian Europe" long after any actual military threat existed.[45] Elsewhere I have argued that something akin to this imagined threat has played a partial role in Germany's largely negative response to modern Turkey's repeated efforts to join the European Community and later the European Union.[46] This is not at all meant to imply an unbroken chain of political animosities, cultural prejudices, and discursive practices over hundreds of years in multifarious circum-

xxi

stances. But when those Germans who disapprove politically of dual citizenship for Turks also feel "threatened" by the prospect, which Turks do they really have in mind? The local grocer who sells them their vegetables? The accountant who does their taxes? The novelist who writes prize-winning German literature? The teenager riding the bus? The Ottoman soldiers of the fifteenth and seventeenth centuries? German allies in World War I? Their dentist?

The decade that elicited Zafer Şenocak's commentary began not only with German unification but also with the Persian Gulf War in January 1991. It ended not only with the brief prospect of dual citizenship for Germany's resident Turks but also with renewed military hostilities between Iraq and the United States (and Great Britain), and with ongoing grave tensions among Muslims, Serbs, and others in the Balkans. Seen against this backdrop, the ways in which Germans imagine themselves as Westerners and Europeans in the 1990s, interacting with Muslim populations at home, in Europe, and elsewhere in the world, take on broader—if no less diffuse—contours.[47] Obviously, not all Muslims are Turks, and less obviously—to many Germans—not all Turks are Muslims.[48] In contemporary German parlance both terms are often made to stand in for something different (un-German, as it were), disquieting, even exotic. The design of Şenocak's *Atlas of a Tropical Germany* thus alerts us to something that cannot be reduced to a "mere" political dilemma that arises when large numbers of people migrate to the Federal Republic from a place presumed (by Europeans) to be outside Europe (and hence *exotic*). A "tropical" Germany is also one imagined to be fundamentally affected—not quite its familiar self—when something "tropical" resides within its borders. This gesture on the author's part should, I think, be understood in two ways. On the one hand, he addresses some painful prejudices that sometimes shape German attitudes toward Turks. Along these lines, one might conjecture that the fall of the Berlin Wall in 1989 has left more than one imaginary wall intact. The "wall in the head" between East and West Germans has a lesser known cousin, a sturdy wall of symbolic bricks between Germans and resident Turks.[49] On the other hand, to speak of the Federal

Republic as "a tropical Germany" is also to say that these and related categories—of them and us, self and other—are wholly inadequate to the task of understanding Turkish-German relations today. A Germany fundamentally affected by the lived and shared presence of something "tropical" within its borders is itself a tropical land. As concepts, "inside" and "outside" become nonsensical figments of imagination; spatial relations are perhaps not what they seem to be. Furthermore, how one thinks, speaks, and writes about Turks in Germany is not a matter of politics and imagination alone, but also of language.[50] Another "tropical" concern that propels these essays is the discourse (or rather, discourses) about Turks in Germany. What are the figures of speech, what are the "tropes" that confine the image of Turks to a "tropical" realm? And by the same token, what kind of language would be capable of mapping a world that Turks and Germans share? What kind of language would be capable of inhabiting that very shared quality?[51]

When Şenocak calls for "a new shared language"—as he does, for example, in his essay "The Concept of Culture and Its Discontents"—we should bear in mind that the piece was originally written in September 1993, less than a full year after the fatal fires of Mölln and Solingen. As tempting as it would be to read this as a familiar clarion call for intercultural harmony and understanding, the critical thrust of his formulation points to something different. One political scientist has organized an extensive study of "changing attitudes" toward national security questions among (West) Germans around "the dynamics of generational change."[52] For Şenocak, too, albeit with different emphases, generational shifts are crucial to grasp. Again, this may be understood in two ways. First, the experiential and imaginative points of reference for the first generation of Turkish immigrants (de facto immigrants) are not—indeed, cannot be—the same for the second, third, or subsequent generations. This seems sensible enough. Yet common presumptions of intractable cultural differences between "Turks" and "Germans" in Germany are often predicated on the assumption that generations do not change, that what was thought to be true in the 1960s must be even more true in the 1990s, now that so many more people are involved. Born in 1961 in Ankara, Şenocak himself speaks as a member of the second generation of Turkish immigrants, having moved to West Germany with his parents in 1970 and acquired German citizenship only as an adult in 1992 (and only after repeated attempts). More pertinently, though, his rejection of seamless generational continuity indicts a structural flaw in an outdated map of Turkish-German culture. This flaw has to do with the second kind of "generational" shift that he has in mind. For the new life experiences of those who immigrated as children and came of age in Germany also generate new cultural maps. This is not to say that members of the second generation merely trade one national culture for another as they move from one country to another. (Nor does it mean that any previous maps, including those of the second generation, apply to the third generation.)[53] But it is to say that their compass points of orientation are not exact replicas of those that guided their elders. Something else is going on. These essays from the 1990s ask what this something else might be; at the same time, they are an indication that it is taking place. Şenocak implores his readers—Turkish and German alike—to recognize the structural newness of this historical juncture, the shared quality of which is no less new for Germans than it is for Turks.[54]

If this historical moment in Germany needs to be mapped along different coordinates from those that have gone before (and to which we cannot help alluding as we try to understand what is happening now, even though we will find no adequate answers there), then the imaginative lines of affiliation for the so-called Turkish diaspora must also be redrawn. From Şenocak's perspective, Turks (in any country) who think and act as though Germany's resident Turks either are or should be a mere extension of the Republic of Turkey and its national political concerns fail to recognize that Turks in Germany no longer simply live in another country. The essay "Germany—Home for Turks?" speaks to this: "Changing one's location without simultaneously changing one's perspective leads to a vacuum," one that cannot be filled with "the phantasm of the lost homeland." In this Şenocak takes aim at several targets, including political organizations, representatives, and media—German and Turkish, in Germany and in Turkey—that find it easier and in some cases politically more desirable to deal with Germany's resident Turks as if they composed a "little Turkey" in Europe.[55] This tendency to wrap presumed "cultural difference" into tidy packages that can then be assigned to isolated, clearly delineated spaces or enclaves is further undermined by Şenocak's invocations of other places and other times where "difference" is hard to locate (in the literal sense of this verb).[56] Occasional allusions in his essays to Seljukian Anatolia and "Moorish" or Andalusian Spain might be seen in this light. These references to premodern Turkish or Muslim dynasties, where deserts bloomed and what we in today's jargon would call multiculturalism flourished, serve as a reminder that tolerance and diversity do not "belong" to Europe as a delimited geographical space.[57] They are part and parcel of Islamic history. Historical figures such as Ibn Rushd (Averroës) and Ibn Sina (Avicenna), great and greatly influential Arab-Islamic philosophers whom readers will also encounter in Şenocak's reflections, remind us as well that the Islamic world has long been part and parcel of European thought, Enlightenment, and humanism.[58] But if a world of "cultural difference"—so often presumed to prevail between Turks and Germans today—cannot be tied to a fixed point in space or time, then how much more creative must we become to recognize the life world that they share or the shared histories of their culture? One might say that Şenocak's essays inaugurate this creative project, which also has vital implications for political and analytical alternatives.[59] They certainly promote it.

In effect, the author urges his readers to cultivate a kind of sixth, historical sense, "a history of Orient and Occident touching each other."[60] Conjuring a stubbornly predictable trope—"Between Orient and Occident"—in the title of one of his essays, however, he actually undermines the very notion of "betweenness" rather than shoring it up. For if we imagine that we can draw a line around the space "in between," as if it were a place of ambiguity surrounded by places that were themselves not ambiguously fluid but thoroughly settled, then we cannot begin to picture the cultural entwinement of Orient and Occident. Difference does not reside "between" these supposed polar opposites; it is already a constitutive feature of each point along a spectrum of cultural relations and historical transitions. From this vantage, the author writes in "The Concept of Culture and Its Discontents," "opposites are no longer discernible as such." Given the tenor of our times, it should come as no surprise that this contradicts with manifest urgency the status often ascribed to Islam in Western and European cultures. Reflecting on Turkish-German relations beyond national unification and de facto immigration, Şenocak also has the end of the Cold War in mind—a historical moment, he observes in "War and Peace in Modernity," in dangerous search of a "common enemy." As his portrait "Salman Rushdie between the Fronts" makes clear, Western cultures are not alone in chasing a stick-figure enemy, easily sketched in two dimensions. But those who rely on an agonal trope of civilizations whose "clash" is gloriously foretold render themselves incapable of seeing anything that might lie "beyond petrified fronts."[61] By this, the public intellectual who has authored these essays does not mean that conflict is merely an optical illusion, or harmonious living within easy reach. What he does suggest is that the Turkish-German "encounter" (Şenocak prefers the word "touch") poses a particularly fruitful challenge to the model of enemy camps qua enemy cultures that Samuel P. Huntington finds so compelling. The politics of Turkish-German relations cannot be grasped without recourse to cultural questions, in Şenocak's view, but neither can a wide range of political conflicts be reduced to alleged cultural differences.

This is the vein in which we might, for example, best understand the essayist's striking comparison between an American scholar such as Samuel P. Huntington, associated with the Olin Institute for Strategic Studies at Harvard University, and Botho Strauss, the playwright-novelist who is arguably Germany's most talked-about recluse. Likening these two disparate thinkers in "War and Peace in Modernity" (1994/1998), Şenocak zeroes in on one notoriously controversial essay by Strauss, first published in February 1993 in Germany's most widely read weekly news magazine. When "*Anschwellender Bocksgesang*" was reprinted one year later in a collection of essays on German identity by right-wing intellectuals, the flames of public scandal were fanned as many leftists and liberals clamored to assert that the hitherto rather apolitical writer had now taken an openly "fascist" turn.[62] Although Şenocak does not take up this particular question, he rejects Strauss's apparent nostalgia for "the bosom of German tradition." Like Huntington, Strauss too averred in 1993 that "conflicts are approaching that can no longer be appeased in terms of economics."[63] Faulting both for their allegiance to conceptual paradigms that stem from the past and bypass the present as they try to predict the future, Şenocak nonetheless finds that the German misfit is more realistic than Huntington in one crucial regard. Where the latter sees the threat of explosive confrontation primarily in rigidly antagonistic cultural terms (where "non-Western" civilizations supposedly stand in for one cultural identity and "Western" civilization for another), Strauss sees a decisive fault line running not between cultures but throughout them, as a "conflict between modernity and antimodernity."[64] In this sense, then, Şenocak's reading of Strauss's German nation and Huntington's global stage serves as another foray into "a tropical Germany." This is a place that is perhaps not a place at all, but a moment in time, where cultural rifts, political conflicts, and even historic opportunities cannot be measured or mapped by surveyor's hand.

How then does one chart such a transitional moment, which defies cartographic conventions? Şenocak's methodological repertoire tends to the eclectic, with some familiar markers pointing to the need to know more, rather than lulling us into the comfort of ready answers. Among these touchstones, three modes of thought and orientation stand out. The first might be loosely described as post-structuralist, with special emphasis on philosophers and critics who themselves highlight the expressly political effects of language and discourse. Michel Foucault immediately comes to mind, and the essay "What the Does the Forest Dying Have to Do With Multiculturalism?" begins with an explicit allusion to the French theorist's seminal work on discourses of sexuality, as Şenocak calls for comparable rigor brought to bear on discourses of migration. Edward W. Said's emphatic postcolonial critique of Orientalist discourses in the service of Western imperialism and Eurocentrism is also key, notably when Şenocak challenges the treatment of Islam in German media and politics.[65] But a second leitmotiv is decidedly psychoanalytic in its homage to Freud. "The Concept of Culture and Its Discontents" echoes Sigmund Freud's famous treatise of 1930, *Civilization and Its Discontents*, in its discussion of what the very idea of "cultural conflict" represses. References to unconscious processes and uncanny phenomena also figure prominently throughout Şenocak's essays on contemporary German culture as it deals with Turks who live in Germany and inhabit German culture, too. Finally, a third trace of influence more than hints at the Frankfurt School of Critical Theory, especially as represented by Theodor W. Adorno and Max Horkheimer's momentous *Dialectic of Enlightenment*, written during the years of exile that these social philosophers spent in the United States. Besides citing directly from their chapter on anti-Semitism (in the same essay that he begins with Foucault), the author of these Turkish-German commentaries wrestles repeatedly with present-day tensions between myth and reason, between irrational fears of the Other and rational discourses that want to situate cultural difference safely outside the self.

All these theoretical touchstones notwithstanding, these essays cannot be said to undertake a sustained engagement with any of these schools of thought or methods of analysis. They are touchstones only, suggesting possible directions for further consideration, not paving the way with instructional conviction. Throughout, Şenocak stresses a kind of vibrant mindfulness that should prevail when no prototypes exist that could fully account for Turkish-German relations at this unique juncture. This applies to cultural prototypes and methodological templates alike. When he proclaims in 1990, in "Germany—Home for Turks?," that "the younger generation of Turks in Germany has a historic opportunity to overcome the crisis between

Orient and Occident that has plagued Turkish identity for over a century," he is thinking of unprecedented developments on which a shared Turkish and German future will turn. "We have no concepts for the emotions and psychic structures to which recent historical ruptures have given rise, no concepts for the disarray of the new arrangements," he writes in "What Does the Forest Dying Have to Do with Multiculturalism?"

This attention to things that still lie just beyond our conceptual ken puts the writer at odds with the predominant approach to understanding Turks in Germany today. Whether conservatives cast relations between Germans and Turks in terms of excitable conflict or liberals prefer to cultivate them on the basis of desirable dialogue, Şenocak chastises both xenophobic animosity and xenophilic solidarity, to the extent that they allow only for an encounter (*Begegnung*) between Self and Other (*das Eigene und das Fremde*). This sense of facing each other across a firmly entrenched dividing line does not and cannot begin to accommodate the author's perception of a shared culture and history, indeed, of self and other as already inextricably linked. Even well-intentioned and publicly staged attempts at "understanding the Other" rest on pinning the other down *as* "the Other." For this reason, he opines in "The Poet and the Deserters," "something like a negative hermeneutic could perhaps provide a way out." For many readers, of course, a call for less understanding rather than more is bound to seem counterintuitive. But Şenocak's plea for "something like a negative hermeneutic" that might act as a curative for "the wounds of communication" ("Beyond the Language of the Land") takes aim only at a particular kind of understanding, one that feigns interest in the Other while keeping "it" steadily at bay, imagining it always outside, unrelated to the Self. The reference to a negative hermeneutic should therefore not be mistaken for a blanket rejection of all hermeneutic philosophies, which have taken many different twists and turns since the eighteenth century.[66] To Şenocak's way of thinking, the sort of hermeneutic approach to the Turkish minority that thwarts rather than fosters more profound understanding of the current situation is one obsessed with "intercultural" exchange or dialogue. How can a culture engage in dialogue with itself when it does not recognize itself sitting across the conference table?

To say that Turks and Germans living in the Federal Republic inhabit a shared culture and a shared history, and to say that this particular constellation is unprecedented, is also to raise a question about a different minority, one that has played a preeminent role in German history. Where are the Jews on the atlas that Şenocak charts? The image of healing "the wounds of communication" appears in one of the essays inspired by the great German and Jewish poet Paul Celan, surely no casual coincidence.[67] But readers will look in vain for ready-made prototypes for sociological comparison here, too. While some social scientists may be inclined to draw certain analogies between Jews and Turks in Germany in order to interrogate the merits of assimilation and the dangers of discrimination, Şenocak's imaginative project is not propelled by direct analogy or comparison, certainly not by these alone. Instead, one might say that on this score he posits yet another kind of *Berührungsgeschichte*, a history of "touch" among Germans, Turks, and Jews.[68] One simultaneously poignant and pointed example of this can be found in his "Thoughts on May 8, 1995," written in the context of many public events in unified Germany commemorating the end of World War II in Europe and the liberation from fascism fifty years earlier. If, as the author strongly feels, Germany's resident Turks must enter into a conscious and conscientious relationship with a vexed German history, whether they are citizens or not, then how exactly is this to be done? From what vantage point and how might they contribute to the "paths of remembrance" that Şenocak deems so vitally necessary for a legitimate German future, one that dare not forget the burdens and lessons of the past? What are we to make of such uncanny irony when a German writer of Turkish descent reflects so thoughtfully on the need to remember sagely and responsibly, not by formulaic rote, at a time when a more famous member of the German literary guild reaps applause (and controversy) for appealing to more innocent

German memories, untainted by knowledge of the onetime future that is now the German past? To be sure, when Şenocak mentions Martin Walser by name in "War and Peace in Modernity," the reference is to an alienating image of Turks invoked by the latter in 1993, not to the controversy incited by Walser's polemics on Auschwitz in 1998.[69] But which author offers greater insights into the German nexus of past, present, and future? For understanding this nexus at the century's turn, Şenocak's *Atlas of a Tropical Germany* is, in any case, indispensable reading.

Encountering Paul Celan as an imaginary guide on the byways of this atlas is more than a reminder of weighty legacies from the past. For Şenocak's appeal in "Which Myth Writes Me?" to a negative hermeneutic, "which critically interrogates what is presumed to be understood," is also fundamentally about the limits, mysteries, and marvels of language. This is a call to poetic language, a mode of articulation that creates more labyrinthine ways of knowing time and space, that rescues them from the poverty of dualistic coordinates but makes no pretense at redemption. In part, the essays on Celan represent an engagement with German Jewish experience, but they are also more than that. Şenocak's figurative aphorisms in "Beyond the Language of the Land" revolve in almost dizzying quietude around language, land, and home. But rather than confining language to land, or even suggesting that language becomes a land or a home, the German Turkish essayist brings the very incommensurability of language and land into view. This is also an indictment of the spatial coordinates with which the proper "place" for Turks in German culture and politics is customarily circumscribed. Such objection to perceptual and discursive conventions also foregrounds the elevated status of literary language versus expository prose. Seen in this light, Paul Celan, Salman Rushdie, and other creative writers weave in and out of these essays in comparable manner, inasmuch as their art provides access to multicultural and otherwise complex experience in ways that theory and politics cannot.[70] This then accounts as well for the stylistic mixture that one finds in some of the essays included here. "The Island," for example, presents "a historical place that has become an imaginary site." Coming eerily in and out of focus, the paths we are invited to traverse tickle and tease our imagination as we wonder, like the essayist and narrator, where we are and where we are going. "Does this path lead to the future or to the past?" The imaginative spaces of contemporary German culture, politics, and history that Şenocak attempts to chart throughout these essays mark a place for critical thought. Readers are urged to go where statistics and demographics alone yield neither insight nor orientation.[71]

"People are curious to know where I come from. Few are interested in the path that I have taken," Şenocak writes in "Territories." In this essay and such others as "Which Myth Writes Me?" and "The One and the Other Child," Şenocak cautions us not to confuse the writer's personal background with his writing myth, not to mistake biography for genealogy, and not to imagine that biography and culture are commensurate terms that stand in for or even explain each other. These are all categories of perception into which migrant authors, especially those of Turkish descent, are all too often expected to fit. For this reason, I have sought to trace here some lines of thought that will assist readers as they meander along Şenocak's critically and sometimes urgently creative paths of orientation. Yet American readers are likely to want to know a little more about the Turkish immigrant and German citizen who writes such a tropical atlas, who muses in "Germany Is More a Language Than a Land," an interview conducted in Turkey, "Perhaps I have a Berlin inside me that is located close to the equator." Educated as a very young child in Ankara in the 1960s, Zafer Şenocak also attended elementary school in Munich after moving to Bavaria in 1970 with his mother, who was a teacher, and his father, a freelance journalist. After completing his college-track German high school degree (*Abitur*) in 1981, he continued his studies at the Ludwig-Maximilians-University of Munich, where he concentrated on German literature, politics, and philosophy until 1987. The early 1980s marked the beginnings of the migrant literature in German that grew out of the international experience of "guest workers" and other foreigners in the Federal Republic, and these were also the years when Şenocak began to publish his lyric poetry.[72] For his creative talents he was awarded the Literary Prize of the City of Munich in 1984 and an Adelbert von Chamisso Prize (for foreign-born authors of German literature) in 1988. Together with Eva Hund, he translated an important novel by Aras Ören, an older and more established author of the Turkish émigré experience who lives in Germany and still writes in Turkish (*Eine verspätete Abrechnung* [A belated settling of accounts], 1988). Turning his translator's craft to poetry as well, Şenocak published German translations of Yunus Emre, a fourteenth-century Anatolian mystic, and Pir Sultan Abdal, a melancholic Turkish folk poet of the sixteenth century. Able to survive as a freelance writer and journalist since 1987, he has resided for most of the last decade in Berlin, quickly becoming one of the most sought after commentators on Turkish-German relations at the intersection of culture and politics beyond the national unification of 1990. Cofounder of the international literary journal *Sirene* [Siren], he appears frequently on television and radio in Germany and has lectured throughout Western Europe.

Although he first became known for his poetry in the 1980s, two volumes of essays that appeared in the early years after the Wall signaled the unmistakable emergence of a dynamic new voice in the German public sphere, which itself was grappling with contemporary quandaries between a national past and a European future. Many of the essays made available in English translation for the first time here are taken from those trailblazing anthologies, *Atlas des tropischen Deutschland* (Atlas of the tropical Germany, 1992) and *War Hitler Araber? IrreFührungen an den Rand Europas* (Was Hitler an Arab? A crazy guide to the edge of Europe, 1994). Together with the prominent German political scientist Claus Leggewie, Şenocak co-edited a rare bilingual set of essays on German Turks in 1993 as one kind of collective response to the lethal attacks on Turks in Mölln and Solingen.[73] Between 1994 and 1997 he oversaw the production of a "multicultural" page for Berlin's alternative daily newspaper, *die tageszeitung* (*taz*, for short), to which he was a regular contributor for many years.[74] In mid-decade he published his first collection of short stories, *Der Mann im Unterhemd* (The man in the undershirt, 1995), which inaugurated a literary series of prose writings. *Die Prärie* (The prairie) followed in 1997, and the author's first novel appeared in 1998 as *Gefährliche Verwandtschaft* (Dangerous relations).[75] More essays, poems, and literary prose are currently underway. While a writing fellowship in 1996 at the Feuchtwanger Society's Villa Aurora in Los Angeles (Pacific Palisades) and several stints as writer-in-residence at American colleges have brought Şenocak physically to this country's shores, some of his essays and poems have already been translated into French, Spanish, Catalan, Dutch, Hebrew, Urdu, and Greek.

Most recently, his work has begun to appear in Turkish translation in the Republic of Turkey. A volume of poetry first published in German in 1987 as *Ritual der Jugend* (Ritual of youth) has been available as *Gençlik Ayinleri* since 1994. Three years later a publishing house in Istanbul (Kabalcı Yayınevi) printed Turkish translations of *War Hitler Araber?* (*Hitler Arap Mıydı?*) and *Mann im Unterhemd* (*Atletli Adam*). Because of the growing international audiences to whom Şenocak's provocations offer coordinates of interest and, possibly, orientation, one of the pieces included for English translation here is an interview conducted with the author in Istanbul by Halil Gökhan for a Turkish readership in 1994 ("Germany Is More a Language Than a Land"). The need for mediation between Zafer Şenocak and his new readers in Turkey underscores the fact that this was not the audience for which his writing was originally intended. The Turkish diaspora is no mere extension of a Turkish homeland, at least, not on Şenocak's atlas of a world in flux. At the same time, following his lead through the byways of a tropical German landscape demands new approaches to understanding what it means, not only to be German, but also to tell the story of German history and to imagine the contours of German culture.

Yet how can we be asked both to "risk a renaissance of universalism" (in "Between Occident and Orient") and to "heal the wounds of communication" (in "Beyond the Language of the Land"), to resist the illusion of understanding difference but also to know more about the culture of the Other? Şenocak does call for all these things, some of which may seem contradictory. But the essays gathered here point the way, not to understanding cultural difference, but to understanding culture differently. The "universalism" that their author has in mind is not about assimilation to uniformity or obliviousness to conflict. He asks his readers instead to shift their focus to the manifold shared qualities of a volatile moment in time, a crucial pivot point in German, Turkish, and European histories. The questions he raises and the inroads he makes into public debate are some of the hinges on which a shared political future will turn. Because these essays reflect on different stages and facets of an ongoing historical process in which they also take active part, they are presented here in chronological order from 1990 to 1998. "Germany long ago became part of us German Turks," Şenocak observes in his conclusion to "War and Peace in Modernity." "Now a question is being posed that we cannot answer alone. Are we also a part of Germany?" Given the tropical atlas that he has drawn for us, this is both a rhetorical question and a pressing political one as well. This guide through the Federal Republic's first decade of unification ponders an unprecedented present with the knowledge that a particular future is neither decided nor inevitable.

In conclusion, some editorial remarks on my translations may forestall avoidable confusion. This introduction has incorporated and explained most of the references to things in the essays that some readers in the United States might otherwise find unfamiliar. The notes to the introduction also contain many useful bibliographical references, with an emphasis on material that is readily available in English. Only in relatively few instances will additional explanatory notes (in my voice, unless otherwise indicated) interrupt the flow of the essays themselves. While Şenocak's commentaries stand on their own merit and represent the author's own views, readers may find it helpful to consider these editorial "coordinates of orientation" before proceeding to the essays. In cases where an English word or phrase does not fully capture the nuance of the German expression used by the author, I also provide the German original parenthetically in italics. Occasional information in brackets, on the other hand, entails minor clarifications beyond mere translation. Because the author sometimes uses "Orient" and "Occident" with and sometimes without quotation marks, I have remained faithful to his choices rather than streamlining my editorial usage. The same applies to the upper- and lowercase options for other and Other. Readers will encounter both, which reflects the details of the German original. Where the German text uses the masculinist pronoun "he" for abstract references in the third person singular, I have for the most part adhered to the author's stylistic convention, which is still common in Germany but less so in the United States, where many readers have come to expect writing that is gender-neutral.

One cluster of words that are especially difficult to translate from German into English, and all the more so in this Turkish-German field, has to do with the status or quality of being foreign. Not surprisingly, two words and their respective derivatives figure frequently in these commentaries. The German word *Ausländer* means "foreigner" in the legal sense, that is to say, someone who does not hold a German passport. At the same time, the term is often used colloquially in a nontechnical sense to denote persons with an ethnic, national, or racial background that situates them, in the eyes of the speaker, "outside" German culture and society. This tends to blur distinctions between xenophobia and racism. The German word for the former is *Ausländerfeindlichkeit*, which literally means "hostility to foreigners." Common parlance therefore uses this term to categorize attacks on people who are foreigners in the legal sense, but it also uses it in conjunction with violence against German citizens who are also, say, Turks or Afro-Germans.[76] Standard terminology thus reinforces the misperception that people who ostensibly "look different" are in fact not Germans. Şenocak's discussion of German politics makes many references to these issues, and the translation of *Ausländer* is rendered as "foreigner." Things get more complicated when the author introduces other relevant words that can mean "foreign" or "strange" in a nontechnical sense. *Fremde* is a collective noun for people who are strangers or otherwise do not seem to fit in. *Ausländer* and *Fremde* are sometimes used interchangeably in German, but their meanings and connotations are not the same. Because Şenocak deals with a tangle of legal, political, cultural, and social concerns, he uses these and associated terms to highlight several different dimensions of Turkish-German relations. There is also the adjective *fremd*, which one might use to describe feeling or being "out of place." German has a well-known capacity for abstraction, and consequently I have also had to translate two abstract terms that stem from *fremd*. *Das Fremde* suggests something that is considered strange, whereas *Fremdheit* denotes an abstract quality of being strange. (Interestingly, Şenocak does not use the phrase *die Fremde*, which implies a location in space where one is not at home, usually outside one's home country.) Because these essays chart a thoughtful path through a web of relations between seeming strange and being foreign, I have tried to echo this sense of entwinement in my translations. This is why readers will find *das Fremde* translated as "that which is strangely foreign," for example, or *die Fremdheit* as "strange foreignness." Both terms appear in Şenocak's critical Turkish-German reflections "Between Orient and Occident." The author's unusual configuration of this "between" now invites your engaged curiosity.

To My Readers in the United States

In Germany one often speaks of "American conditions" when the effects of migration on society are being discussed. Despite forty years of experience with immigration, which has resulted in 7.5 million persons of foreign origin residing permanently in Germany, questions and concepts of multiculturalism have remained controversial here. The multicultural society that is already part of official social policy in immigration countries such as the United States, Great Britain, and the Netherlands appears, to many Germans, as a scenario of horror. Visions of something like a "Los Angeles syndrome" fill their heads. They see the threat of ethnic conflicts, the impoverishment of urban areas, the overthrow of their intact German world by foreign elements. Behind these fears lurks the vision of a homogeneous ethnic community (*Volksgemeinschaft*) of Germans, a community to which strangers are granted temporary access at best. Although West Germany subscribed to a democratic constitution after World War II and developed an exemplary system of social pluralism, the country has nonetheless inherited the Romantic idea of a *Volksgemeinschaft*, an idea whose origins predate the National Socialist regime by far. In the consciousness of Germans, genealogy, culture, language, and *Volk* form one unit.

There is a German people (*Volk*) that defines itself ethnically, but is there a German nation that can also be multiethnic? The problems of the German nation-state have often been described. One speaks of the belated nation. According to the literary scholar Karl Heinz Bohrer, "The German people has not succeeded in becoming a modern nation because it never adequately universalized its concept of *Volk*."[1]

As long as Germany was divided and the Federal Republic eked out a quasi a-national existence under the umbrella of the West, the

question of a German nation-state was of only secondary significance. Since unification, that has radically changed. A sovereign,
united Germany must address its role as a nation-state in a Europe
engaged in its own unification process.

The concept of nation is directly related to the question of immigration. For the unavoidable question is this: Who belongs? And
under what conditions? It can come as no surprise when questions
about citizenship law are often at the core of debates in Germany
about multiculturalism. And yet in recent years a second line of
debate has developed, one directly related to visions of a homogeneous society and fear of heterogeneity. Again and again the German
media depict the Turkish population—with more than two million
human beings, the most powerful of the immigrant groups—as incapable of integration, even as undesiring of integration. The Turks are
stigmatized as forever strange. Even for this vantage point the question arises: Why is it so difficult to accept heterogeneity in society?
Especially since the Turks in Germany behave relatively inconspicu-
ously and their demands are extremely modest and cautious. But
even their existence is taken as grounds for unrest. Urban areas with a
high percentage of Turkish residents are viewed as problem zones.
Although there is nothing in Germany comparable to American
neighborhoods with an ethnically homogeneous population, one
speaks of ghettos. It is precisely the diversity, the multicultural activity of neighborhoods like Berlin-Kreuzberg, that frightens many
citizens and politicians. They mourn the German ghetto that has
been broken open, transformed into a colorful state of confusion. Of
course the colorful state of confusion is not a world without problems. The atmosphere is not marked by one jubilant celebration after
another. There are tensions, social conflicts, economic straits. But
must these conflicts always be grasped in ethnic terms? In Germany
these conflicts seldom have ethnic foundations.

If Germany wants to secure its long-range position in Europe and
the Western world, it will have to change its understanding of what it
means to be German and its understanding of itself. This transformation, from a state defined by blood lineage to a modern citizens'

republic, is inevitable for yet another reason. The problems of an ethnically and culturally heterogeneous German society cannot be solved in any other way. This transformation is rich in tensions.

The essays in this book were written over the last ten years. They attend, almost exactly, the time that has transpired since the fall of the Berlin Wall. You might think of them as a kind of taking stock of German reunification, a description of Germany on its rocky road to becoming a modern nation, in a united Europe.

ZAFER ŞENOCAK

Atlas of a Tropical Germany

Zafer Şenocak & Bülent Tulay

Germany—Home for Turks?

A PLEA FOR OVERCOMING THE
CRISIS BETWEEN ORIENT
AND OCCIDENT

To the extent that it took place at all in the shadow of current events in the GDR and in Eastern Europe, the discussion about the new foreigners' law in the Federal Republic of Germany was conducted for the most part without involving us, the second generation of Turkish immigrants. For this law continues to ignore our reality. Having been born and reached adulthood here, we can hardly identify with the law's operative concept of "foreign fellow citizens" (*ausländische Mitbürger*). We can no longer imagine a future in this country that fails to recognize us as German citizens. Until now, however, the authorities have doggedly avoided this decisive question.

Even for the majority of Turks, above all for the first generation, there seem to be more important topics than the security and equality of their future in Germany.

The media and public opinion of Turks in Germany are extensions of Turkish media, Turkish public opinion, and Turkish consciousness. Until now Turks in Germany have had no stance of their own, no vision.

This might not be anything to object to if we were not already in the thirtieth year of immigration and if it were not high time to think about granting citizens' rights to Turks in Germany.

As a result of the labor immigration that led to the phenomenon of the guest worker, the Federal Republic has become a de facto land of immigration for the majority of foreign workers and their families. A second generation of foreigners has grown up here, and a third is already being born. But legislation and even the vocabulary of public discussion limp along behind the existing situation. For years the broad majority of the population has spoken of the "integration of foreign citizens," while the Left has spoken of a "multicultural society." Unfortunately, the discussion exhausts itself in the mere mention of these slogans! Nowhere is it made clear what a profound change of consciousness must take place for all those involved in order for native and future German citizens really to live together successfully.

UNLIMITED CITIZENS' RIGHTS

"We already have a multicultural society," say some. By this they presumably mean cultures and perspectives existing side by side without touching each other. Everyone should be blissful as he sees fit, keep his eye on his own plate, and make himself comfortable in the ghetto.

"Integrate," say the others. By this they mean nothing short of absolute assimilation, the disappearance of Anatolian faces behind German masks.

But can there be an integration for Germans of Turkish origin who have decided to live their lives in Germany if they are not granted unlimited rights of citizenship?

Fellow citizens without citizens' rights—in our opinion no democratic state can sustain such a situation over time without social conflicts and tensions. One must not overlook the fact that there are forces, even in the ranks of the ruling parties (CDU/CSU), that regard even those "foreigners" who have been living here for decades as an alien threat that they would much prefer to get rid of if this could be done legally and economically. These forces, which do not shy away from waging atmospheric battles, benefit from a widespread, undifferentiated view of foreigners. At most one differentiates among different degrees of strangeness: "the greater the strangeness, the greater the danger."

Grotesquely, the view from the Left presents a mirror image of this. Those party congress participants who vote for a general right of residency for every foreigner who comes here are not blessed with an advanced capacity for differentiation or sense of reality.

Demonization and glorification of things foreign lie close together. Both are defensive mechanisms that rest, not on a relationship of partnership, but on one of domination.

When we speak of a comprehensive change in consciousness, we mean that it is time to take up a long overdue discussion of repressed problems of identity and fears of contact. The Turks must finally speak up to situate themselves anew, to orient and define themselves. This holds above all for the so-called second generation and the coming generations. They are the real foreigners because their glance in the rearview mirror is blocked; they live without a homeland or rights of citizenship. And yet they are often not even perceived as foreigners because their language, their appearance, and their patterns of consumption scarcely differ from those of the Germans in their age group.

Is Turkey still their home, then? Can it be the home of their children?

We have the good fortune, which unfortunately often goes unrecognized, of living in a time when concepts like fatherland, home, and nation can be seen from different perspectives and when they no longer function as key words that fit only one certain lock.

Among the young Turks in Germany there still prevails that spirit that only bemoans a split identity, that is to say, speechlessness. They write an endless book of memories, in scraps of childhood, in lost languages or languages not yet found, and the pages remain empty. They have not yet found a language that they could use to translate this book and share it with others. For their fathers and mothers they are the lost generation. Will they be, for their own children, those without speech? Is there a way out of this passivity, out of niches, ghettos, and half-truths?

The birth of German citizens of Turkish, Islamic origin also puts Germans to the test. The tolerance of some Germans for integration seems to have exhausted itself even before integration has begun. The Turks are stigmatized as the ever foreign.

But even the diametrically opposed position, which sees in every foreigner a better human being, which thinks it must accept every archaic custom, every foreign habit, leads in the end only to a tangle of conflicts. For even this position thinks it can get away without changing its own consciousness, without needing the other. But change and contact are key words for a multicultural social perspective. There are paths that must be explored to overcome latent as well as blatant fears of contact, to break out of the ghetto, and to create the atmosphere that will allow the strange and the intimate to be in constant touch, in order to allow something new to grow—a process that can be pleasurable but equally painful, like rubbing a wound. In many ways this process is like creative work.

CRISIS BETWEEN ORIENT AND OCCIDENT

The younger generation of Turks in Germany has a historic opportunity to overcome the crisis between Orient and Occident that has plagued Turkish identity for over a century. Yet these young Turks must not be guided by the psychologisms of today's society in Turkey.

Already the next generations will no longer stand in between, but right in the middle of a European context. Changes of location and perspective are mutually constitutive. Changing one's location without simultaneously changing one's perspective leads to a vacuum. The break with the original homeland took place long ago. But it is also imperative to grasp this break in all its consequences before the empty space to which it gives rise can be bridged.

More often than not the interests of Turks in Germany are a mismatch with those of Turkey. The disenfranchisement of Turks in Germany manifests itself not only in the denial of citizens' rights by Germans but also in Turkey's claim to be the sole legitimate representative of Turks in Germany. In order to realize their capacity to formulate and perceive their own interests in the future, in order to speak their own language, the Turkish youth of Germany must rid themselves of their parents' allegiance to authority and reject a one-sided orientation to Turkey.

Turkish youth must not cling to the phantasm of the lost homeland.

4

MULTICULTURAL—BUT HOW?

Almost all associations that Turks in Germany have founded have their roots in Turkey. That is not unusual if the interests of the first generation are considered. But will it suffice for the future? The German citizen of Turkish origin needs his own face, which must abide differences. For even adaptation cannot prevent him from remaining the other, the one who is different. This difference forms the foundation of his new, perhaps dual identity, or more precisely, his identities!

We must say farewell to an all-too-common notion of unbroken identity. Identity has meant and continues to mean a drawing of boundaries, a resistance, and all too often the destruction of an other. It is no coincidence that Hans Mayer's book on outsiders (*Außenseiter*) attests to the failure of the Enlightenment in a bourgeois society that excluded and marginalized those who were different and strange.[1]

A new concept of identity that would allow us to live together without having to sacrifice difference and personality on the altar of identity would need to have gaps through which what is different and foreign could come and go. Identity would then not manifest itself as hegemony. Whether this remains a pious hope or becomes reality someday probably depends on whether we learn to accept differences and to shape them productively, whether we learn to touch each other.

A comprehensive change of consciousness must take place, a reorientation that links the Turks with Germany's problems and perspectives, that enriches the Germans with the cultural legacy of the Turks, and that finally grants the second generation the space it needs to find its own way.

Precisely in these fields of tension, in the contradictions of two cultures, in the conflict between modernity and tradition, the Turks of Germany can cultivate the kind of creativity that leads to a distinctly specific culture. They will hold their own roots in awe as something strange, and they will make the strange land their own. No mummification of ancient identities, but a brilliant negotiation of standpoints and perspectives.

But German society, its cultural life, its curricular programs in the schools, all this needs to change. A society's multiculturalism cannot exhaust itself in satisfying needs for exoticism and folklore. Rather, it must lead to a serious encounter with the culture, language, history, literature, and religion of those who are different. Of course this is especially crucial in the arena of formal education in the schools. Today's discussion about the future of the multicultural society barely acknowledges initial signs of moving in this direction.

IS HISTORY CATCHING UP WITH US?

The consciousness of individuals and the collective unconscious always have a longer breath than administrative measures and legislative periods. For unlike these short-term phenomena they are guided by symbols and metaphors that are thousands of years old. For this reason it will be crucial to explore where, how, and why different cultures that have tried to live together have failed in the history of civilization. We have not yet digested the bitter experiences of the twentieth century!

But who among us, Turks of the second generation in Germany, has concerned himself in real depth with Germany's past and its future?

Doesn't immigrating to Germany also mean immigrating to, entering into, the arena of Germany's recent past?

The history of Jews in Germany—the history of the largest minority of another faith—and the creative influence that this history had (but also the effect of the Enlightenment on Jews, with all its consequences, including emancipation and assimilation), all this offers us an experiential background that we have not yet analyzed. Even the bitter experiences that led to the [near] annihilation of the Jewish minority in Europe must be reflected upon in the conception of a multicultural Europe.

But doesn't an anti-Islamicism, dug out of medieval mothballs and restyled for the present, threaten to join the anti-Semitism of European history? The era of depoliticization, short-lived concepts, and postmodern arbitrariness has been followed by a neoconservative phase that makes nationalism and xenophobia socially acceptable again.

Without question most Germans have successfully been integrated into the European process since 1945. Nonetheless, the so-called German question still touches a nerve. This is less a question of borders than one of German national feeling, German identity.

The Germans, especially those in the West, have banished their national feeling into the unconscious. This too was part of a strategy of "coming to terms with the past" (*Vergangenheitsbewältigung*), which should more properly be designated a project of forgetting. Aside from formulaic reconciliation and commemorative events, the ritual of overcoming also includes the suppression of moods, the sublimation of emotions, embedded in the total concept of reconstruction, which didn't exactly take the thorniest path.

As the French philosopher Alain Finkielkraut impressively describes in his book *Remembering in Vain*, this ritual of overcoming actually prevents the realization of memory and encourages the bravado of forgetting.[2]

The presence of a historical, cultural, and religious minority could prove to be an important corrective in the process of rediscovering a new German national feeling. Obviously this situation also harbors an enormous potential for conflict. And because conflicts build up and are fueled by the unconscious, action must be taken now.

NO INTEGRATION WITHOUT CITIZENS' RIGHTS

In the thirtieth year of immigration, Germany must no longer be last in line in Europe when it comes to the rights and life options of foreigners. Despite German assurances to the contrary, we see no serious desire for integration as long as the debureaucratization and the liberalization of the German naturalization law and its implementation are excluded from discussion.

The offer entailed in the statement "The foreigners could become citizens if they really wanted to" remains a mockery in the face of many aspects of German citizenship that derive from genealogical criteria. According to these principles, someone of German descent from an Eastern European country, whose ancestors might have lived for as many as five hundred years outside German territory and who speaks only broken German or no German at all, is considered a German. But not a Turk of the second or third generation who speaks far better German than Turkish: he is and remains a foreigner. The fact that racialized thought (*der Rassegedanke*) can continue to play such a central role in a country where such thinking led to unimaginable crimes is, to put it mildly, alienating.

ISLAM AS A EUROPEAN FACTOR

The fact that German citizens of Turkish origin are simultaneously German citizens of Islamic faith seems to give rise to growing fears of contact.

Islam has long since become a European factor. In Germany, for example, there are nearly two million Muslims. Unlike other countries in the European Community, Germany does not recognize Islam as a legitimate religious community in the public sphere.

The future will show whether extremist positions on all sides will yield to a dialogue or whether they will further encumber the consciousness of those involved. After anti-Semitism, Islam must not become a new target for European self-definition. Muslims must also work against this. They must finally begin to consider their tradition critically. This means not only tolerating freedom of expression but also encouraging it.

Islam doesn't force itself on anyone. The true nature of this religion is more tolerant than one might easily think in light of so much fresh violence and arbitrariness in the name of Islam.

The roots of Islam's tolerance lie in its history, not in a glorified utopia, but in the everyday, lived history of a Moorish Spain, a Seljukian Anatolia. The time is long since upon us to take up and further that critical Enlightened spirit, which determined Oriental thought from the ninth to the thirteenth centuries, brought a high civilization to flower, and decisively influenced the European Middle Ages en route to modernity.

Humanist ideals and Enlightened thought did not derive from Europe's own. They are, rather, twilight creatures of West and East, coproductions. Practicing and cultivating them would not be alienating for Muslims. On the contrary, this would be the discovery of a lost Muslim tradition.

This rediscovery and recultivation of Muslim tradition in the critical light of pluralism will be possible only for those who have learned to change perspectives, to consider what is strange as one's own and what is one's own from a distance. And only therein lies the chance of the coming generations to deal differently with prejudice and stereotypes, in order to eliminate them—perhaps, one day—from the language of humankind.

January 1990

Was Adolf Hitler an Arab?

ON THE LANGUAGE OF EXPERTS
WHEN CONFRONTED WITH
BLANK SPOTS

Since war broke out in the [Persian] Gulf, they show themselves almost daily on the screen. The experts. Sitting in front of the regional map with a ponderous, weighty facial expression, they interpret the mysteries of this unfathomable conflict. Every day they span anew veils between "Orient" and "Occident." Only they know the slits through which the other can be espied and comprehended, the other who is so different that we cannot grasp him with our rational system of thought. Behind the experts a line already forms, of all those who would also like to cast a glance through this slit or who have already done so: travelers, adventurers, enthusiasts, business operatives, world politicians, almost all of them of the male gender, united in the one, unmistakable way of looking at the Other, the Impenetrable. That which appears behind the expert so casually (*gewöhnlich*) as a map, with cities, names of cities, regions and national borders, actually harbors something altogether different from just any region of the world. It is a magnetic field for fictions. A blank spot, inhabited by beings who come into focus only when the experts look at them.

The synchronicity of inequality enables the expert—and through him, all of us—simply to turn back the dial. In this sense he serves the function of a shaman. Death sentences seem plausible, wars can be waged, despotism and tyranny are virtually a law of nature. And Enlightenment? Humanism? Yes, our expert knows precisely how relative these concepts are. He knows that the Others neither strive for nor merit such achievements. At the efforts of naive Westerners to convert the eternally archaic Orient, he can only smile. Whether a renewed attempt with a modernized colonialism could prove worthwhile? That would be a good audience question sometime.

The expert must constantly translate. He does so by distancing himself. The farther away from his object he is, the better he understands it. The distance also makes it possible for him to repress all the elements in himself that could remind him of the Other. The demonization of the "Other," the "Other" that is always also violent, renders violence exotic. One's own capacity for violence is repressed. An Enlightened European can of course not be Saddam Hussein. But was Hitler an Arab?

Karl May and Goethe already knew best who Kurds and Persians were.[1] Were they also similarly well informed about themselves? But the expert believes he knows the Other better than himself. And in order not to lose himself entirely in the Other, he needs distance. "I understand his language," he says, "but only when it is completely different from my own." Sword-swinging, death-conjuring fundamentalists are easiest for him, not so much the individual but the masses. The masses speak the language that he knows best without having to differentiate. It is not his own language but that of his alter ego. From there he can set his chains, plant his genealogical trees, paint characters and typologies. The Old Man of the Mountain and Khomeini, Saddam Hussein and Saladin [Salah ah-Din], they are all directly related.[2]

And the bureaucrat from Ankara? The bourgeois Iranian in Parisian exile, who can talk for hours about French wine without mentioning the Prophet's commandment? They are both absent from the expert's view; consequently he does not talk about them. Why does he not understand their language, which after all is his own? Perhaps *because* it is his own? Representatives of such groups are in his eyes at best the Westernized elite, with no connection to their own people, alienated and condemned to failure. But is this not precisely the opinion of religious fanatics who want to exterminate those who think differently?

The expert so perfectly masters the language of his "Other," of the fundamentalist, that it is often enough identical with his own lan-

11

guage, without the expert realizing this. In front of the maps of mysterious regions, his chair does not wobble as long as his view of the Other does not lead him to himself, and as long as the "Other" does not notice him behind the slit in the veil, does not discover his "Other" in him.

January 1991

"Orient" and "Occident"

AT THE CROSSROADS?

When you take a step in my direction, I take ten steps in yours, and when you come to find me, I run to meet you.—Muhammad

Understanding is when one develops what another has spoken out of oneself.—J. W. v. Goethe

A Muslim cleric condemns an author to death because he believes that the writer has vilified his religion in a novel.[1] An unruly crowd burns the book at demonstrations and demands the head of the condemned.

At the same time another book enjoys a record-breaking publication run in Germany. In this book an American woman who is married to an Iranian describes her moving battle for her daughter in the realm of Islamic fundamentalists.[2] The story is told in the style of a dime novel, peppered with pointed defamations of the Iranian people. The victims, mother and daughter, represent the world of the West; the daughter's father is the perpetrator, an Iranian, one of a million potential executioners who take to the streets to demand the head of that other author.

There is no question for which side the heart of the civilized, enlightened world beats. The strong, emotionally charged reactions to these two completely different books demonstrate that the cultural conflict between Orient and Occident, which is founded on massive prejudices as well as mutual ignorance and contempt, is in full swing. It probably marks the beginning of a larger conflict between North and South.

Nothing indicates that the war that has now broken out in the Near East will lead to a transformation of consciousness in the West

13

and in the West's relationships to the states and peoples of the Near East. Rather, even the modern Western world and its politics have landed in the apparently still powerful force field of myths, symbols, and images of epochs gone by. In the West's language of propaganda the aggressor from Baghdad is not merely a power politician acting on the basis of nationalist and economic interests, just as European states themselves still thought and acted until recently. Instead he is an irrational and bloodthirsty Oriental, a Saladin who has gone forth to strike fear into the heart of the Occident.

Analyses and attempts at explanation again and again emphasize this difference of the Near East and the modes of thought practiced by the human beings who live there (who are mostly Muslims). This approach appears indispensable to European identity, as it after all distracts attention away from the threatening insight that it is not only the dictator from Baghdad who represents the type of the Oriental tyrant, not only this dictator who thinks and acts irrationally. Rather, Western statesmen, fighting ostensibly for Enlightenment and freedom, do so as well, their airplanes shot down by their own weapons systems exported abroad. Yet the process of Enlightenment can in truth not be completed, even in Europe, because human beings need to wrest rational, independent thought from their drives (*Triebe*) repeatedly. Their Enlightened capacity for reasoned majority (*Mündigkeit*) must be won over and over again anew, individual by individual, generation by generation.[3]

On the other hand, Saddam Hussein—until recently still an acknowledged outpost of the secularized modern world on the front line against rising fundamentalist Islam—assumes the posture of a holy warrior who wants to hitch all Muslims to the chariot of his nationalist politics. In the Near East, however, much more is at stake than regional dominance, than oil and large power interests. Beneath the current conflict there smolders a cultural conflict that has lasted for centuries between "Orient" and "Occident," between "Land of the Rising Sun" and "Land of the Setting Sun" (*Morgenland, Abendland*).

Communication between "Orient" and "Occident" will remain disturbed as long as the West refuses to understand itself as part of this communication system, with all the projections, wishful thinking, distorted images, imponderables, and irrationalisms that this millennia-old discourse entails. That is to say, in all the systems that are currently operating and whose roots extend far back into the history of civilization, into antiquity, the roles are fixed. Here, the perpetrators and those who are active; there, the victims and those who are passive. The realm of good in battle with the realm of evil, the uncanny darkness, chaos. Reason (*Ratio*) versus irrationality.

In this context the new role of "United Europe" is especially disappointing so far. On the surface it has been barely visible in this conflict, yet in the background Europe is actively involved in the culturally conditioned misunderstandings between "Orient" and "Occident."

This ambivalent attitude emerges especially clearly in Turkey's failed attempts to become part of this united Europe. Certainly, there is much to be said against an immediate or imminent Turkish membership in the EC [European Community], from the country's difficult economic situation to its uncertain democracy, which evidences many deficits. But to date the Europeans have failed to send a generally positive signal for the future and to pave the way for reasoned optimism (*eine Perspektive zu eröffnen*). The really tragic thing is that Europeans apparently have still not understood at all how indispensable Turkey's involvement in European processes is for discourse with the Islamic world, have not understood at all that Turkey is the sole secularized country with a Muslim population that has been oriented to the West for a century. Because of this it is only rational to consider the democratization, the economic upturn, and the stability of Turkey among the unshakable interests of the West.

Now that the West is once again relying on Turkey's support, comments by respected European politicians on the other hand sound foolish when they define the EC as a Christian club. In doing so, they not only exclude Turkey but also suppress the Jewish and Muslim minorities who are citizens of Europe.

This would all be difficult to understand were it not for an age-old, deeply seated fear of the Turks. The Turkish Peril (*Türkengefahr*) is not something that was taken care of three hundred years ago before the gates of Vienna. It has a ghostly presence today in many heads, leading to artificial acts of holding oneself aloof, scorning, rejecting, and showing no interest in anything that has to do with Turkey. This ghostly presence leads Europeans to ignore everything that does not fit into their familiar prejudices and categories.

While the media overlook no opportunity to go on and on about Islamic fundamentalism in Turkey, the political strength of which corresponds roughly to the potential for right-wing extremism in France, the high numbers of women who study or teach at [Turkish] universities are, for example, not accorded much interest. Even modern Turkish literature—which turned to urban themes a long time ago, operates within the discourse of European modernity, and also concerns itself directly with identity issues affecting Europe—is not acknowledged. If at all, preference is given to publishing those authors who deliver picturesque images that seem exotic from a European perspective, for example, the representatives of village literature.[4]

Who desires a united Europe that merely varies its images of the enemy: yesterday Jews and communists, today Muslims? Who wants a Europe that despite horrific historical experiences has learned neither how to deal with minorities nor how to discourse with the Other, with that which is strange? Perhaps such lessons are so difficult because they concern a secret brother who has been cast out. The hinterlands of Turkey are close in Berlin-Kreuzberg, in the same house. The slogan that proclaims multicultural European society remains a placebo as long as the current patterns of identity remain intact, and as long as the diversification of modern complex societies and the uncertainties (*Verunsicherungen*) that result from them are met with increasingly simplistic incantations.

Even if Europeans, in their fixation on a rigid, uniform model of Christian-Occidental identity, have repressed the fact today—just as the peoples of the Near East have repressed it, because of their colonialist trauma—Orient and Occident belong together. They form one indivisible unit. The fruits of the Enlightenment were planted and cultivated jointly, in Andalusian Spain and in Seljukian Anatolia, in the Córdoba of Averroës [Ibn Rushd] and in the Konya of the mystic Jalal al-Din Rumi.[5]

In contrast to the universal idea of humanism and Enlightenment, the excesses of modern technology, the absolute claim by humans to domination over nature, and Europe's colonialism are fundamentally particularistic (*ureigen*) advances. Criticized more and more by Europeans themselves today, they threaten all of humankind.

But a reversal, which would also be in the interest of Western societies in the long run, is possible only through a change in the structures of communication between cultures and religions. Nonetheless, a public critique and working-through of colonialism has not yet begun on a broad, societal level. It almost seems as if the Germans were mastering the past for all peoples. In fact, the special guilt of the Germans, which must not be denied, has distracted our attention away from the crimes of other European nations. For example, who still speaks in France today—and how do they speak—about the one and a half million dead in the senseless colonial war in Algeria, about the human rights violations committed by the French soldiers then?[6] One does not have to dig deep in European memory to bump up against violence and horror. It suffices to go back thirty years and look just outside the gates of Europe! Most Britons believe today that they are conducting a just war in the [Persian] Gulf. What role did the British play in this twentieth century as a colonial power in half the world?

Could it be that united Europe wants to steal away from this bloody history?

In addition to open and critical discussions about the past, the transformation of thought also requires the renunciation of illusions and fixations of identity, that is, fixed notions of who one is and is not, and who the other consequently is and is not. As Edward Said—a Palestinian-born American scholar of literature—demonstrates so impressively in his book *Orientalism* [1978], "the European" has been encountering "the Oriental" for at least three centuries only by way of the mediations in his head, the stereotypes and images that "Orientalism" has created. The Oriental is typed and classified, custom-

17

made for advantageous use (*Umgang*). He combines, for example, fears and violent fantasies, yearnings for physicality, sensuousness. The Orient appears at once as sensuously excessive and cruel. These projections destroy every inchoate attempt at communication and recall anti-Semitic images of "the Jew" in Europe.

Under completely different sociopolitical conditions, of course, Islam for a long time enabled peoples and cultures to coexist peacefully in the Balkans or on the Arabian peninsula. It developed a tolerance that permitted even the theological authority of a Sheik-ul-Islam, the highest-ranking cleric, to sing the wise praises of forbidden wine in verse and to scorn the crowd in the mosques as hypocritical. Yet this Islam is being increasingly reformed from within to function as a militant ideology that is on principle hostile to dialogue. To be sure, whoever knows Islamic history very well knows that a perversion of this faith is underway here, one that can perhaps be explained as a reaction to the colonialist aggressions of the West and the psychologisms of Westernization in Islamic societies. In any case this perversion will leave irreparable damage behind.

The masses of the Near East are extremely insecure. These are human beings whose personality is split; inferiority complexes dominate their dealings with what is foreign to them.

A ruler of Saddam Hussein's type seems to confirm in a downright fatal way the stereotypes that are traded in the West about the Orient and Orientals. It is as though the human beings in this relationship between "Orient" and "Occident," a relationship shaped by domination rather than partnership, were adapting themselves more and more to the images that the others have of them, as if they were, so to speak, approximating their typology. The toll that this then exacts means nothing less than the extinction of their personality.

"Orient" and "Occident" stand at the crossroads. Either they will find the path to a new understanding and coexistence, which is above all also in the interest of peace in Europe, especially with regard to Muslim minorities. There are also precedents for this in history, even though they have been largely repressed today, driven out of shared memory. Or they will follow the path to a new barbarism, into a cycle of mutual disdain and destruction. Their shared history also yields more than enough examples of this.

It is Europe's responsibility today to recall shared roots and to build bridges. But similarly, Muslims should self-confidently recall their Enlightened and liberal traditions in order to shed the strait-jackets of the regime of violence, in order to find their own way out of the burning crisis of identity.

Or will we all prefer to prepare for future slaughter by donning again the suits of knightly armor to simulate in video games Crusaders and holy warriors?

February 1991

The Island

Where had Hauptmann buried his box of notes? This question pre-occupied me when I went to the island. I knew that the old man—because of his photographs one knows him almost only as an old man, even though he attained world renown already in his youth—had spent not only his summers but also the end of his life here.[1]

From Berlin the train ride takes three hours. A span of time, the very least that one requires to say good-bye to the city, jostled on all sides, and to establish a relationship to the brittle peace peculiar to the landscapes of the north. The ascetic qualities of this peace can drive the most intense couples apart.

The Baltic Sea city that the train approaches, which seems half asleep, half abustle on a Saturday afternoon, is not yet the end of the line. You are lucky if you arrive on a Saturday afternoon and the streets are already empty. It is raining. In the dejected atmosphere, traces of bustling activity, the sun that now and then peeks its head through the clouds, the noisy operation of restaurants off in the distance, and the suburban amusement park have an involuntarily odd effect.

Only when one recognizes one's own basic mood in the city's indecisive dejection (*Tristesse*) does one seem to have completely arrived. This dejection will decisively reject every change, no matter how small, as a disturbance of the public order, of the peaceful coexistence of peoples, and of familial bliss.

The city is radiant with an unreal quality that can turn into aggression at any moment. In one shop window there are picture books and *Heimatliteratur*; in another, books on foreign-language pedagogy, dictionaries.[2] A book series with the title *How Does It Work?* Looking things up in order to get away, all the while standing with both legs on familiar ground. Dreaming in cue words.

20

To reach the island, on whose shores children still dig for amber today—in past centuries, patricians and representatives of the rising bourgeoisie tried their luck for the sake of this stone, usually in vain, by acquiring the island with all its living and lifeless souls, its mobile and immobile goods—to reach this island, one must continue the journey by ferry.

The people whom one is meeting or leaving are waiting. The island's inhabitants are waiting for the change that has long since seized the mainland. But ideas often need more time than people do to cover a certain distance.

Nonetheless—it is arranged. The travelers that come expect a few nice days in the past. Back into the past by a few years, and one is already erecting castles in one's memory, barricades of time that doggedly assert themselves against anything short-lived and fleeting.

Every intruder is assessed with suspicion. And in response to questions that are unexpected or deemed intrusive, windows and doors are closed and locked. No one home, they say.

From the landing dock everyone moves backward. The larks trill. A look scrutinizes the neighbor. While the travelers move backward from the landing dock to mingle among the lives that the dead have laid down—only in this manner do they as strangers reach the village—they run, the island's inhabitants, forward, run ahead of their own lives, with glances fixed on the future. They load their thoughts and dreams onto kites that they let fly along the main thoroughfares of the island.

Everyone here can trill. One is proud of descending from birds. Even today everyone is a little sick from scurvy.

Even today everyone has a note from Hauptmann, a few pieces of amber in a can in the kitchen cupboard, and a love affair in progress.

Where is Hauptmann's box of notes buried? Is the entire place one single museum? A castle in the air, made of repressed thoughts?

Only black cats know the way to the dead. And they can't be tricked. Did Hauptmann like cats?

Capitalism is the dessert of socialism, says the man who rents out bicycles. When actually all one really wanted was to return the bicycle. No word at all about getting any money back, a missing part, broken brakes, a defective light, or anything like that.

According to this view, fascism was the appetizer to the main course—for forty years the brothers and sisters sat at the table and no one got really full; they saved up their hunger, which sooner or later had to be transformed into aggression. Now it was done. Dessert is served. Apple tart with raspberries.

Every morning one awakes with a headache. It is as if the wind had pulled all one's teeth. One lies, shivering all over, in bed. Slowly, one learns to hear again, to distinguish the nightingales from the larks. Slowly one also learns to smell again. Salt. Salt in one's lungs activates memory. One recalls: the opposing directions of those who were running forward and backward. Perhaps one had already asked the decisive question on the first morning or saved it for the return trip. How is it that those running forward and backward don't run into each other somewhere? They are all running in a circle after all, in other words, in the same direction.

The town council has a newly arrived fax affixed to the gate of the town hall. In it Comrade Hauptmann proposes the following solution to all questions pertaining to humanity and the future: The island becomes a free commerce zone. This is to be understood as follows: From now on the island may be inhabited only by people who understand something about socialism—among others, by authors who have at least one book publication, painters whose self-portraits can be recognized by someone without fantasy, the kind of person who prefers "regular" gasoline, beyond this by automobile drivers who are in permanent conflict with the technical inspection folks. To accommodate all the relevant population groups—since they do not exist as individuals—to act favorably on all applications, the island's inhabitants must be relocated. Proposed solution: the West stirs them up to apply for permission to leave.

One challenges them to take paths that avoid encounters with those who are arriving, paths that the black cat takes, paths to the deceased and worn out (shoes and Party members), paths that split whoever walks on them into two parts (or doubles them, depending on one's point of view). One part strives forward, the other backward; one comes with a stomach full from the meal, picking his teeth, the other is a gap in himself between tables set and cleared, a dog without a master. Groups dissolve, couples split, individuals lose their thoughts and dreams. All of them are looking for the path not yet blocked by the department stores' delivery trucks, beyond the main traffic routes. Does this path lead to the future or to the past? Only the drunkards leaning here and there against lantern posts and thick tree trunks show the way. In front of large hotels, bars are hurriedly set up in shacks. Photo opportunities. All the colors have the effect of forced gaiety, as if they had something to hide.

The travelers moving backward now have a longer way to go. The island's inhabitants, on the other hand, barely need to step out their door to move ahead. The future races toward them.

They will not meet. On the large stage that has been set up over the harbor, the bands of the decades are playing, jazz, blues, Beatles, hard rock, and no-future imitations called the Central Committee.[3] Showmen of all the television generations perform, as in a competition to fast-forward through everything ever missed. Shoulder to shoulder, they move without touching each other. Their shoulders are padded. Everyone focuses inward. No weeping will be audible anymore and no trilling.

In the steamboat taking off, old folks sit and hide their faces behind newspapers, pocketbooks, and handkerchiefs.

Everything was merely a conspiracy of the guests, they say. At night they gave each other secret signals with flashlights in the trees, they say. They dug up Hauptmann's notes, they say. They surreptitiously followed the black cat, they say. A long path through the darkness, to the highest point, from where the descent begins.

How does one recognize in such a time where one belongs? By the coffee cups? By the brand of cream for one's coffee? By the chocolate? Once it was the color of one's hair and eyes, and the shape of one's nose. The length of paved streets, the number of villages with electricity.

Think of Hapsburg, the Imperial Eagle, the church, the faith, the

Immaculate Conception, Icarus, the Wright brothers, and socialism, which inherited something from everyone without giving birth to anything new. There is something obscene about everything that ends, like a knife that disappears in a sheath. The ceremony of disguise goes by the name of melancholy. The end was settled on a long time ago; nonetheless, it must take a surprising turn every time, an unexpected twist (*Einbruch*). The end must not be a consequence. In the end, developments bring ruin to every belief that one holds.

A tear opens, a chasm, an abyss. The other shore becomes unattainable. Without a sound the grief over what has been lost and the joy about what is anticipated mix indistinguishably, against a coarsely patterned background, a historical place that has become an imaginary site, as if they were entering into a complicated relationship, long desired and strictly forbidden.

August 1991

What Does the Forest Dying Have to Do with Multiculturalism?

Much as Michel Foucault has changed our understanding of sexuality in Occidental societies, we need to study the discourse of migration in Europe and scrutinize its practices.[1] Talk-happy media have taken to commenting on the phenomenon of migration in an inflationary way. The complexity of concepts and their internal contradictions disappear in dubious simplifications. Even in scholarship and especially in public discussion, there is a widespread assumption that, on a planet crisscrossed with communications networks, virtually immune symbols that define cultural differences could still exist. In the current discussion this leads to concepts being taken as a point of departure that are incapable of grasping and expressing the complexity of the entire situation or the intricacies of the details. In other words, no archaeological work on concepts is taking place. One speaks of *foreigners, naturalization, integration, assimilation,* the *second generation,* and so on. But all these terms convey different realities, in keeping with different perspectives. Even if this society were willing to understand itself as a society of immigration, what it would demand of immigrants—what it would be prepared to give and to take—remains completely open.

Heiner Geißler's sketch for a multicultural society—one that would take its cue from economic and demographic necessities and be held together by the concept of constitutional patriotism—is a first step toward addressing the situation today.[2] Unfortunately, even Geißler relies on the static images that mark the majority's encounter with foreigners, rather than conducting empirical analyses about the immigrants' state of consciousness and their symbolic universe. These static images would have us believe that Turks harken to monotonous Turkish music and prefer lamb to pork. And they are also entitled to do so.

Many questions remain unanswered because the speaker is not able to think in different languages, that is, to think in terms of the standpoints and interests of his objects and addressees. His point of departure is not interest in the culture and specificity of the others, but the plain economic necessity according to which Germany and Europe again and again require a new supply of labor. But will numbers and external factors suffice to create a society that allows the participants to know each other's perspectives and symbols, to bring them into contact with each other, and thus to set new identities and identifications in the place of those that are crumbling?

In Germany the end of socialist utopia and rapid unification have created the illusion that current events and contemporary phenomena can be described with nineteenth-century language, with concepts such as *nation* and *Volk*. We have no concepts for the emotions and psychic structures to which recent historical ruptures have given rise, no concepts for the disarray of the new arrangements. The ones that are used are ripped out of context. Façades of ruins.

In public discussion the concept of a "multicultural society" belongs, even more than the concept of "the forest dying," to a conceptual framework that pairs understanding with repression. While discussion about forests dying took place in the middle of society— because the problem concerned everyone directly—discussion about a multicultural society happens on the periphery, with no noticeable influence on practical politics. Those who are strange (*Fremde*) are per se marginal groups, even if their strangeness is not always cast in terms of socioeconomics. Their passivity and powerlessness are a fundamental condition of their existence. Every time they try to break out of their role, they encounter not only the power of the center but also the firm will of those marginal figures who want to stay on the margins, who come like day trippers from the center to look into the depths for a while. The day trippers from the center borrow the marginal feeling of those who are strange and foreign (*fremd*), those who supply THE OTHER and a projection screen for yearnings that the day trippers have. These strangers will not succeed in breaking out unless they engage in fundamental debate with those

26

from the center who are invested in establishing minority. If the feet are bound by the chains of resistance, the hands are bound by the chains of solidarity.

The majority of the center would like to distance itself from the margin, to cast it out. The minority of the center wants to preserve the margin as margin, to conserve the margins. In both cases distance and its preservation are essential. The majority of the center distances itself from the margin. The minority of the center identifies with this distance. Everything strange must be preserved at any cost. Even understanding that which is strange would already diminish its allure. Because of this there are hardly any efforts to question and to analyze modes of behavior. That which exists exists as if it were a law of nature. Things have always been as they are now, and things as they are now will always be so in the future.

Every relationship rests on differences and similarities. If the similarities disappear behind the differences, a dialogic relationship collapses into the stigmatization of the other. Language is used to speak no longer with one another but only about one another. Those who are strange express themselves now only in their symbols. Head scarves, circumcision and wedding celebrations, talismans, extended families, mothers-in-law, men's honor, wedding dowry . . . The problem of integrating those who are strange becomes a problem of perception. The perception of the stranger rests in turn on a disabled (*verkrüppelt*) concept of strangeness, on a restrictive model that recognizes only assimilation or ghettoization. In each case the point is to avoid any contacts that could provoke change. The tension between self and others (*dem Eigenen und Fremden*) must be maintained at any cost.

The majority of the center and he who has assimilated, the ghetto and the minority of the center, they all speak one and the same language to distance themselves. But reality is syncretistic. It is the reality of mulattos, of bastards. Reality is taboo.

When symbols of strangeness that could be pinpointed are at stake, the other religion plays a key role. The discerning rationalisms of modern industrial societies allow for faith only as fortress or as

27

nothing. Galloping changes in the external world are accompanied by only a creeping change in the human soul, perhaps even less. Perhaps a desperate force tugs wildly at an immovable rock. Every modern religion seeks to rescue the soul, which is without words, from the onslaught of words outside. Christianity has come the furthest in adapting to new circumstances because the European secularization process has promoted it the most. Islam, on the other hand, still carries those mythic elements that irritate and also unsettle modern human beings. This mode of faith can exist only in the ghetto, to the extent that it stigmatizes modernity as devil's work and is perceived by modernity as the dark, uncharted part of human beings, forced into the deepest layers of consciousness.

It is remarkable that Islam, which at its core most certainly has strongly rationalist elements, should appear so irrational in today's diaspora. What role does the stigmatization of this religion play in its seeming implacability? Is it not the case that images of Islam as a closed, fanatic, and threatening force more and more frequently lump all Muslims together, including the secular and critical among them, and lock them into this restrictive and hostile perspective?

Religious dogmatists like the fringe position.[3] They need the stigmatization in order to define themselves as OTHERS. They have taken leave of the process of Enlightenment, of reasoned majority (*Mündigkeit*), and human emancipation. Rationalist, late-industrial society reminds them of their own ritual, mythic remnants, displaced into the subconscious. Citing the psychoanalytic theories of Sigmund Freud, Theodor W. Adorno [and Max Horkheimer] concluded in an essay on anti-Semitism, "Those blinded by civilization experience their own tabooed mimetic features only in certain gestures and behavior patterns which they encounter in others and which strike them as isolated remnants, as embarrassing rudimentary elements that survive in the rationalized environment. What seems repellently alien is in fact all too familiar."[4] It becomes a projection screen for fears and yearnings.

In this regard the preservation of all cultural identities that are supposed to provide the foundation of a multicultural society appears in a completely different light. The pressure to assimilate exerted by the majority corresponds to a counterpressure, exerted by the minority, to preserve. This counterpressure is usually circumscribed with terms such as *cultural independence* and *identity*. In both cases the participants take as their point of departure the illusion that their respective identities are unbroken and easily distinguished from each other. The Muslim becomes the stranger per se. The minority represents society's potential enemy. The agenda becomes not to recognize this minority but to expel it.

September 1991

Translated by Judith Orban

Tradition and Taboo

All the taboos of a culture revolve around *topoi*, around the fixed measures of one's own identity, details of pictures and letters of a text.[1] The quoted, fragmented, broken-up text is praise of discord, the body split in two, a spell upon totality. The text toys with those coordinates of identity, built up as power, destroys positions and points of view. Text as an injured tongue. Does the injured person love his wound, his cut tongue?

How much familiarity do we need in a foreign place? How much of that security, that state of being embedded in the legends, myths, configurations of beliefs shared by a people, a sphere of culture?

Stories of prophets, legends of saints couched in a mother tongue that has been pushed into the background, into the role of a second language, these stories displaced to distant, never-seen places known only through photos or dreams. Every strangeling (*Fremdling*) has gone through a coming-to-terms with the mother, but has another such ahead: coming-to-terms with the father. The mother is the guardian of language, of gestures. The father is the keeper of conventions. Father defends the saints from blasphemy. Faith and its prophets. An inner voice holds the strangeling back from blasphemy against his own origin, even though he is filled with rebellion. His inner voice holds him like a chain, until the root has gone numb.

Sooner or later, all feelings die off, together with the numb root. A great deal of pain could be avoided if the root could be ripped out sooner, but it can't be found. What remains after the feelings are gone is the cynicism of the homeless, who travel from one longing to another, ever restless.

Like rotten teeth, the taboos are extracted from the language. A cynic feels no pain. The roots are dead. Nothing is sacred. Fears are banished.

As soon as the taboo grows silent, it is removed. The mother is already dead then.

How many conventions do we need? How much history? How much tradition?

The history of every stranger ends with his birth. That is what distinguishes him from others, who are the writers of their own histories. The stranger is a writer of stories—often only a storyteller—because the spoken word is the writing of the homeless.

In the pursuit of tradition, many a discovery seems ridiculous, many a feeling seems borrowed, some things are only a cloak, which the next one will throw off. There is no inner voice that promises the ultimate silence, a chain for truth, only noise about a simulated past. Flailing arms, the rage of speechlessness, toothless violence. The taboos are extracted teeth.

Show me your teeth and I will tell you where you come from. The locals have teeth filed to points, with sharp edges and solid roots. With the strangelings it's the very opposite. Their roots are sharp and turned inward, cutting into their own flesh. The points are blunt and smooth.

The identified stranger loses all intimacy. Everything must be revealed. History. The chain that will not relinquish him. He becomes the addressee of others. The foe-friend not chosen by himself. He is mired in an absolutism of relationship from which there is no escape.

The white man hates him. The greatest fear of the white man is being without a home country (*Heimatlosigkeit*). The sum of the suffering of all exiles. The sum of all pangs of conscience for all those whom he has driven out. History in the no-man's-land between memory and conscience, forgotten but not yet entirely repressed—never to be entirely suppressed by any institution of oppression or judgment.

March 1992

31

Dialogue about the Third Language

GERMANS, TURKS, AND THEIR FUTURE

The girl from whom I bought newspapers every day when I was in Istanbul once asked me if I was a German or a Turk. When she noticed that I was taken aback by her question and hesitating with an answer, she continued talking, as if she were talking for me:

In recent times many come here in order to learn Turkish.

Turks or Germans? I ask back, in the hope that this will enable me to avoid an answer.

Like you, neither nor.

Or both, I say. After all, I can speak Turkish and read newspapers and books in both languages every day.

And where is your homeland? the girl asked back.

Homeland! Who on earth invented this term, and from where did you get it, I blurted out, although inside I felt calm and even-keeled.

You must be very sad. Are you mad at me?

I am not sad. I live in Germany and am happy there. I grew up there, you know. I know almost every corner there.

Are you here on vacation?

Finally, a question that I can answer, because the answer will be different from the one she expects, I found myself thinking.

No, I am working here. I came here to write a book. A book about the Germans.

A book about the Germans? About the ones that you know or about the ones that you don't know?

That's something I haven't thought about yet. I think that, in general, I know the Germans very well.

Yes, you are of course one yourself. The girl laughed craftily.

I am very happy not to be a German. To be a German in Germany, that is doubly difficult.

What do you mean?

There are many peoples who don't like themselves and who, because of that, start to hate others. But they love their country, the landscape, the air, the climate in which they live. They balance out the hatred in their head with their body.

Like the Turks, countered the girl.

But the Germans can't stand themselves or their country. They hate with head and body. That's why they need distance between themselves and others. A kind of buffer zone. The others usually don't understand it, but that's in their favor. A hygienic zone that keeps germs from crossing over. It's not necessary to fall over each other.

But they travel around the world so much. Even here there are a lot of them.

That's only to show the others how strong and superior they are. Besides, as I already told you, they don't feel comfortable at home. It's much too cold there and full of factories and superhighways.

That's not true at all, the girl protested loudly. An uncle of mine also lives in Germany. He sent me a calendar once. A wall calendar with twelve pages, one for each month. There were many gorgeous, green landscapes with a lot of forests and old churches. I had a strange feeling inside and wanted to go there right away, a feeling like a yearning, although I've never been there and can't stand my uncle.

Can you understand now why I like living there? Germany is a country that one hates from yearning. A yearning that one absolutely has to get rid of. A country in which every type of gaiety systematically turns itself into mourning. For every way of speaking and

33

walking there are clubs and associations, and the state earns money for the belief in God. Just imagine how hard it must be for a German. Everyone envies him for his success and his wealth and the beauty of his country, but no one loves him. He hates the others for what they admire in him. He is like a man unhappily in love, whose desperation sometimes creates something unimaginable and sometimes gives rise to unimaginable destruction. He is lonely.

Isn't it dangerous to live with the Germans? It must be just as bad as with a father and a mother who don't love each other and take it out on their child.

That's exactly what I'm writing about. I'm looking for an answer to the question, How can one like a people that calls itself ugly?

You know, the Germans and the Turks actually get along very well together. They hardly know anything about us, barely take notice of us. We on the other hand know them very well. We play a kind of hide-and-seek. Our relationship is enlivened by an unspoken tension. Yet they suffer from the compulsion to speak about everything until they draw their last. They don't suffer, they enjoy it, especially when they are talking about something that, from their perspective, is outside. They domesticate everything strange with language. In fact, they take notice only of what they put into words. This is how we can protect ourselves from them.

What side are you talking about now?

I'm talking about us and the others. But is that so important? Whether it's us or others, those are just blank spaces that everyone can fill in for himself.

I can't follow you, but I do know that I'm on the side of the Turks.

We are in the process of building islands for ourselves in Germany; we are burying ourselves in our neighborhoods, our familiar routes. We're getting used to the mentality of the buffer zone. Recently I've even started going to a Turkish dentist.

Now I'm really certain that you're a Turk.

34

In Berlin, the city that I come from, we live completely according to the city map. There are districts and areas that we're better off not entering. But among ourselves we are safe; we can touch each other, laugh, and be glad. This established order makes life easy for us. Depending on the game plan, we are sometimes more German than the Germans, sometimes more Turkish than the Turks. Perhaps we are even a little more friendly to each other than you all are here among yourselves.

That's like living in prison!

You're exaggerating. Besides, we don't have any language problems anymore. If we don't learn German, we can be certain that the Germans, sooner or later, will learn Turkish.

If you haven't all forgotten your Turkish by then.

And anyway, is that good for you all if the Germans learn Turkish? You said you didn't want them to know you.

Yes, that would completely overburden them. Then our life would really be in danger. Maybe we, Germans and Turks, would have to learn a third, common language that no one except us would understand. That would make us accomplices. In which every one of us would have to spell out who he is. A language that would inject us into each other like a vaccine and immunize us against each other so that we can be together without hurting each other. A third language, in which our children can tell each other about the beauties of their common father- and motherland, can complain to each other about the love and affection that each side withholds, can come together in cold and warmth without neutralizing each other. A third language crafted from the alphabet of the deaf and dumb, from the broken sounds, a bastard language that transforms misunderstandings into comedy and fear into understanding.

That sounds really nice, she says, but just in case you don't find this language, you can all come back here. Sure, it's getting more and more crowded, but somehow we manage. We just shave off some of the buffer zones. Besides, for all of us, this is our homeland. And

35

if you all can't part from your Germans, just bring them along with you.

For the person who has lost his homeland and tries to go back, the return will be a minor escape attempt in the face of a larger one. That's what I thought to myself without putting it into words.

April 1992

The Poet and the Deserters

SALMAN RUSHDIE BETWEEN
THE FRONTS

Cultures have begun to fall into formation like armies in battle. This began even before the Ayatollah Khomeini issued the *fatwa* against the writer Salman Rushdie.

The Islamic legacy in European culture has been dispelled from European consciousness in spite of or because of its significant influence on the Renaissance. In the twentieth century the Jewish legacy was subjected to the most comprehensive attempt at eradication in human memory.

Arab thinkers, translators, and poets decisively helped shape European arts and sciences—especially philosophy—in the late Middle Ages and in the Renaissance. Is it possible to imagine Thomas Aquinas without Ibn Sina (Avicenna)? Or the critique of church dogma without Ibn Rushd (Averroës)? How were the poets of Provençal and the troubadours related to the Minnesingers of Arabia?[1] Today these questions occupy, if at all, only a small handful of scholars who call themselves Orientalists. In this context important studies, such as *Avicenna und die Aristotelische Linke* [Avicenna and the Aristotelian left] by Ernst Bloch, have been almost completely forgotten.[2] In their stead it has become fashionable to speak of the "Islam Problem." It would appear that Islam threatens European civilization, sentences poets to death, banishes those who think differently, exercises no tolerance whatsoever, and is fundamentally inclined to violence. Isn't this ghostly image, eagerly disseminated even by enlightened media, used to justify the behavior of those who act like crusaders of modernity? Those who even pursue ethnic cleansing, as the current jargon has it, in order to save the Occident from the aggressive reach of the Islamic Orient?

Are the Muslims in Europe Trojan horses? What causes this one-sided, distorted perception of Islamic culture? What explains the blindness that is brought to bear against precisely the enlightened, creative, and critical forces of Islamic cultural circles, even when they live in the middle of Europe, in Paris, Vienna, or Sarajevo?

The importance of reform-minded thinkers in Bosnia, for example, cannot be assessed highly enough. Here, in a cosmopolitan and enlightened environment that evolved over time, a new Islamic understanding of faith appropriate to our times was conceived. The author Smail Balić, who lives in Austria, speaks of a "more intellectual" interpretation of religious sources, of the development of Islam from a religion of law to a religion of attitude (*Gesinnungsreligion*). As his essay on Muslims in Bosnia further details, religiously minded Yugoslavian Muslims take a critical stance toward tradition.[3] They know how to distinguish Muhammad's commands that are bound to a particular time from Muhammad's commands that are generally valid. Balić especially stresses the role played by Husejin Djozo, the modernist theologian who [later] died in the 1980s, who emerged as both a rigorous scholar of Qur'an exegesis and editor of the journal *Preporod* (Renaissance).[4] This journal appears every two weeks and serves as a forum for a modernist understanding of Islam in Bosnia. Europe and the majority of its intellectuals are not only blind to these initiatives, which are so important for the future of all Muslim minorities in Europe. (Today there are more than ten million Muslims living in the European Community [*sic*] alone.) Tragically, European intellectuals are also deaf when these Muslim minorities are subjected, as they are now, to the threat of destruction.

Since the Enlightenment, the Orient has become Europe's shadow, without clear contours, hard to define, comparable to the unconscious. It was Sigmund Freud who, in his theory of the unconscious, likened that which is conscious to Europe and that which is unconscious to Asia.

In this fashion the Orient went from being a real competitor and challenger in the Middle Ages to a source of fantasy and irrational fear in the modern age. In the most favorable case, the Orient inspired the imagination of European artists; in the least favorable case, it mobilized crusades. The tradition of the crusades extends from the Middle Ages into the present, where the Serbian Chetniks [guerilla soldiers] are massacring the Muslim population, also in the name of the Christian Occident.

For the Orient, Europe is not a shadow. A body with clearly circumscribed parameters, it exudes real threats on the one hand, and also exerts fascination on the other. Isn't the unconscious the repressed component of power? The unrest under the mantle of domination and control, an invisible fire that is steadily stoked and finally erupts? The mantle of rationality and Enlightenment that Western civilization has worn for centuries was never intact. The archaic images and symbols of religions and myths, the *topoi* of the pre-Enlightenment legacy, continued to live beneath it.

When cultures march against each other like armies, poets who are worthy of this designation become deserters. They blur the front lines, they are shoved aside, persecuted, or perhaps only misunderstood. But who makes up the army, who are the generals? Aren't the generals those intellectuals in the writing guild who sit on their cemented symbols like statues?

More and more, the language of those who cross borders blurs the boundaries between Europe and the Orient, between Enlightenment and myth. These border violations give rise to a new language that ruptures the images of both cultures and binds them together. To a certain extent this language remains unintelligible in both cultures.

The debate about *The Satanic Verses* has demonstrated that many Western intellectuals have turned into stone idols that worship themselves. They are far removed from grasping the dialectic and tragedy of the Enlightenment in the West, let alone from understanding the significance of Rushdie as an Enlightened skeptic within Islamic culture. For the zealots of Enlightenment, Rushdie's *The Satanic Verses*, this wonderful travesty of identity, is no more accessible than for the zealots of Islamic faith.

On every side of the front, the deserter remains a stranger, a marginal figure whose internment at the same time means his exclusion.

As a creative writer, Salman Rushdie is neither the vanguard of Enlightenment at the gate to darkness, nor is he a pamphleteer who polemicizes against Islam like a medieval cleric. But dogmatists see only pamphlets. A man stands either on the right or on the left. Standing on the light or on the reft is not possible. A man is either right or wrong. The world is divided into true and false, good and evil. By no means is this the case only in American Westerns. Holy texts also follow this pattern, at least according to the perspective of some holy men. Poets who stand on the reft or the light are eyed suspiciously by them. Poets are skeptics; their tongues attest to broken identity. In this state they are ill suited to waging war; they are deserters. If they are not executed and their works not burned, one speaks of a tolerant age.

Modernity is the age of doubt. That strengthens the poets and weakens the saints. Does this explain the wrath of the latter?

The debate surrounding *The Satanic Verses* gives voice to the conflict between the basic principle of the democratic world, "freedom of opinion" (*Meinungsfreiheit*), and the basic principle of totalitarianism, "restriction of opinion" (*Meinungskontrolle*). That this case pits not two secular systems but Enlightenment and myth (in the form of a world religion) against each other lends the situation a special volatility. Yet if one regards *The Satanic Verses* as a literary work, it describes this rift more profoundly and more existentially than any pamphlet for one side or the other could possibly do. Literary experience begins where personal experience ends and one seeks a language for that which cannot be expressed. [...] A writer of Muslim-Indian heritage, born in Bombay, writes English literature, inspired by works of Islamic mystics, pre-Islamic Arab myths, that is to say, with concepts and characters from mythologies that the European tradition either never knew or completely forgot. [...][5]

Rushdie's text destroys literary identities that formed their own boundaries and aesthetic taste by preserving images, metaphors, and *topoi*. Every writer plays with such inherited elements, develops his own personal handwriting out of them, if he wants to be more than an epigone. Someone who crosses borders between languages and cultures, like Salman Rushdie, violates and unsettles commonplaces all the more because he operates at a greater distance from them. Injuries that have been experienced personally are transformed into the injury of language. The rift goes through the tongue. Language attains an expressive quality that often seems to be in constant motion, as only the homeless are. This is comparable to the music of border crossings, flamenco, tango, or rebetika. The rift that goes through the tongue makes irony melancholic and melancholy ironic.

It is no coincidence that books such as *Midnight's Children* [1980] or even *The Satanic Verses* were written by an author whose literary background extends from tales of Islamic mystics, the Qur'an, and Hindu myths to the novels of Occidental literature. The relationship between fiction and revelation, the relationship between poet and prophet, and the broken, distanced relationship to spirituality—all this can be interpreted only against the background of a culture that has for centuries placed a text, that is to say, the Qur'an, at the center of its creative thoughts and acts. In the debate surrounding Rushdie's oeuvre these considerations are no less significant than his talent for storytelling and his penchant for the fabulous, which everyone loves to compare with *The Arabian Nights*.

Theoretical explanations do not render that which is multicultural accessible to experience. But literary works such as those of Salman Rushdie do. They give shape in language to the personal and subjective experience of transgressing borders.

The works of European writers of Muslim heritage give rise to a new aesthetic. By means of ironic distancing, it ties the severed strands of communication between cultures anew. In so doing it renders the repressed components of the Other in the Self accessible to experience again. But will the pillared saints of identity, here as well as there, allow for this diversification of identity? [. . .][6] Does an aesthetic mode of perception exist that understands and mediates the bastardization of European literature? An aesthetic mode of perception that could counter the terrifying ghosts and prejudices that are given such solid shape by the media?

Where "understanding the Other" yields no further inroads,

something like a negative hermeneutic could perhaps provide a way out. We should no longer cast our eye on what we presume to understand, but on what escapes understanding, defies digestion, violates taboos and boundaries. Only then does work like Rushdie's actually begin to take effect instead of being incorporated and domesticated. Ram A. Mall, an Indian philosopher who teaches in Trier, has described the situation to date best: "Enculturated understanding of the stranger is an understanding of the self with a mask, a masked understanding. The understanding subject appropriates the object to be understood by changing it according to the subject's own design and its own prejudices, by arranging the object and raping it."[7]

On both sides, the generals still have the say, and not the deserters.

December 1992

The Concept of Culture
and Its Discontents

One could say that cultures are like trains moving each on its own track,
at its own speed, and in its own direction.—Claude Lévi-Strauss, *The*
View from Afar

When one speaks of "culture," one is always speaking only of oneself.
There are no other cultures. "Culture" is in itself a tautological concept. When cultures are compared with each other, this happens on
the basis of a concept of culture that is a synonym for the person who
looks from himself to Others and distances himself from them. The
concept of culture is bound to a certain perception of the world, of
human beings, and of their history.

When one speaks of "cultural conflict," one has reached the limits
of one's own concept of culture. The gaze that looks at the Other falls
back onto the one who is looking. From the vantage point of one's
own "culture," differences are ascertained that must be removed to
resolve conflict. Otherwise one is threatened with the loss of one's
own identity, or at least with an identity crisis.

In this sense "culture" has evolved in the history of ideas as one of
the most nebulous concepts that language knows. All "cultures" that
have not themselves developed this concept, but wanted to apply it to
themselves, or were exposed to the more or less "forced" choice to
have to apply it to themselves, have failed in doing so. This concept
could neither describe nor develop their view of the world; neither
could it bring their view of the world into fruitful contact (*Berüh-
rung*) with the culture of Others. It led only to a solidification of one's
own standpoints, often on unfamiliar ground, to a binding of identity, which became impermeable and—even where it is supposed to

express self-determination—trafficked in determination by something outside itself. Culture is a circumscription of relations of power (*Herrschaftsverhältnisse*) according to which those in power maintain their positions and convince those whom they dominate to act like them. Thus the desire to preserve one's own "culture" becomes a boomerang. Relations of dependency are veiled behind concepts such as "self-determination" and "cultural identity." One speaks without recognizing that one has no language.

We speak to the Other with our words. We do not speak *with* him because we do not know his words. Perhaps he has no words for the things that we mean. Perhaps the relationship between his words and the things they designate is different from the one that we construe.

For the Greeks of antiquity, those who lived outside Greece—that is, those who did not belong—were barbarians. But what did the barbarians call the Greeks? And what did they call themselves? With the discourse about culture and civilization our sphere, also geographically designated as "West," has created an illusion: the illusion of global, generally human insights. In the abstract, Enlightenment values, such as the concept of human rights, are uncontroversially correct and understandable. Yet we lack the words to communicate these values to others. For we express these insights only in our own language and piously hope that the others will adopt this language. The others are supposed to learn our language because we define the world for everyone. This dissolution of boundaries on our part makes us strong and often arrogant as well. We no longer perceive the other even though he stands before us. If the other wants to communicate with us, he must make our language his own. He must choose concepts that he has not developed. Thus arises a forced dialogue— less a dialogue than a reflected monologue (*reflektierter Monolog*).

Concepts are mirrors into which we gaze. When one speaks, for example, of the "discontent in culture," which culture is meant? The culture that uses this concept to describe itself is distorted when the concept is cited to describe others. "They have no culture" and "their culture is different" are helpless constructions in the futile attempt to situate oneself and others, to create intimacy or distance, or to de-

44

scribe such intimacy and distance. It is as impossible to construct generally valid patterns for human relations as it is for people to drink stones. European civilization believes that relations can be generalized, and this belief simultaneously makes it ill. European civilization has glorified interpretive models of the world, which represent variations, as generally valid, eternal truths.

The objective sciences (*Wissenschaften*) in the secularized world, which have assumed the legacy of monotheistic religions, do not function any differently from their predecessors in this regard. It is not the invisible that they render absolute but the visible. Even if there are skeptics and fringe figures in scholarship, as there were in theistic times with respect to absolute metaphysical truths, the dominant tendency is nonetheless to describe and interpret the world unequivocally. This narrows the spectrum of truth. This is what causes the modern world enormous difficulties in dealing with differences. We stand in the tradition of eternal truths and unequivocal explanations, which are at best resolved dialectically. How can theses and antitheses be thought without synthesis, without immediately being forced into a state of war? If "culture" goes hand in hand with keeping drives in check and dampening aggressive potential, then it relies on certain interpretations of drives. Is Freud's school of thought imaginable without the Judeo-Christian-Occidental school that preceded it?

Meanwhile, the counterfeit coinage brought into circulation with the concept of culture has reached astronomic proportions. For one person, culture means home and provincialism; for another, it means national identity. For a third, it means his sexual identity. For yet another, it means openness to the world; and so on.

The concept of "multiculturalism" wants to lend expression to the simultaneity of diverse cultures. But does the meaning of the word (culture) allow for a culture that is not multicultural? Can there be different cultures at all according to the word "culture"? Or is culture not already a concept that is bound to a certain worldview and time?

From the vantage point of culture there can be, as I have said, no other cultures. The concept of "culture" describes always only one culture, the one from which it itself emerged as a concept. The definition of other cultures as culture already entails a certain way of imagining culture, one that is supposed to be valid for the others too.

There are basically two possible stances one can take toward this state of affairs.

One can make one's own culture, which represents culture per se, the measure of the Others. According to this principle, the Others are equal, inferior, or superior in worth. The universalist perspective, which takes a notion of what is generally human as its point of departure, uses such a definition, as do the particularist perspectives, which rest on the perception and respect of differences.

Or one can say farewell to the concept of culture and not grasp one's own language as the means of dealing with (*Auseinandersetzung*) other "cultures." We and the Others are all equally speechless when we look at each other. Language is created only for our own purposes (*für uns selbst*). It doesn't explain the Other; it makes him appear beyond explanation (*verklärt*).[1] Once we have recognized that our languages are useless, we take our leave of the need to define the Other in order to define ourselves. We do not have to bind him in order to free ourselves. We are forced to create a new language, together with the Other. For this new language we have no textbook. We cannot rely, as in scholarship (*Wissenschaft*), on facts and an imagined objectivity. But even the concept of subjectivity seems inadequate (*untauglich*), since we can no longer define ourselves through the other. That is to say, since we have dissolved our traditional identity. Even the dialectic method, by which we established positions, has lost its usefulness because opposites are no longer discernible as such.

We find ourselves on a journey without having left the place where we stand. It is not our surroundings that are different but we ourselves. We take our leave not only of the concept of "culture" but also of concepts such as synthesis or symbiosis. We turn away from the certainty of knowing that we possess our knowledge only through language, which has gotten away from us.

What is to be done? First of all, we must overcome a fear that the

Other could be somehow superior to us on this score, that he somehow possesses a magic formula, a language for the shared situation that neither of us knows. We are all confronted with a tabula rasa, a situation in which we must regard and express our origin, our memories, our legacy anew. We are mute contemporaries, standing blind in front of the past and recognizing in it only hazy, broken outlines. We must take recourse to communicating with each other with a kind of sign language.

Let us try to be clear about what we have lost with the concept of "culture." "Culture" did not only describe our life habits and contexts, our creative achievements and modes of production. It was the very ground on which these things arose and on which they were able to flourish or wither. It was the expression for a certain way of living. If we want to communicate with Others, who find themselves on another ground, who use another expression or have no expression at all for it, we must confess to our speechlessness instead of insisting on our concept of culture. This is difficult because speechlessness is always tied to loss of power. Without language the Other cannot be met with power. Will the Other force his language on us? Will he alienate us from ourselves? Expose us? Perhaps as having lied? Do we not have to resort again to tools of domination in order to escape defeat? All these thoughts are created by a dialectically cast mode of thought that is concerned with describing world history and the civilizing process not as a constant search for shared new languages but rather as a relationship between rulers and ruled, masters and slaves. Everywhere where history unfolded only in categories of domination, history meant the failure of human beings living together. Those presumed to be the victors were only the shadow of the vanquished. Their power was founded on the powerlessness of others.

When those without speech stand across from each other, they must rely on their senses and their bodies. Their bodies develop a new, immediate relationship to space and thus also to each other. They move and interpret the movements of the Other. They coordinate their movements with one another. They cannot shed the fear of being determined by the Other, but at the same time they are guided by a drive to observe the Other, to recognize him and to know him. There is a process of cognition, at the end of which something like a coexistence of the One with the Other could stand. Recognition, getting to know each other, and acknowledgment are interdependent. They are the physical, pedagogical, and psychological steps in a process that moves inexorably toward the elimination of speechlessness and the development of a new shared language. The existence of the Other, the perception of his existence, leads to the relativization of one's own standpoint. Whoever takes leave of the concept of culture has razed his fortress. He will no longer be able to think of his standpoint in absolute terms, for he is just as naked and untouched as the Other. His orientation no longer derives from the tips of his shoes but from the horizon, the point where this horizon can melt together with the horizon of the Other. He perceives himself, his own standpoint, as only one possible point on the map of the world. No longer does he perceive the world as a point inside himself.

September 1993

Germany
Is More a Language
Than a Land

GÖKHAN: How would you situate yourself and your poetry against the background of home and belonging (*Heimat und Zugehörigkeit*)?[1]

ŞENOCAK: It may be that the poet is a part of his poem, yet where does the poem belong? If you approach the poem as a scholar, then you can assume that the poem belongs to the language in which it was written. A sociologist or a literary scholar interprets the poet in the context of the society, the country, the environment in which he lives. Generally the poet is regarded as a being that has provisionally settled into society. Why is this the case? Perhaps the point of departure for a poem is the moment in which a human being does not feel that he belongs to the world in the midst of which he sees himself; the poem is the echo of a dissonance. In the poem I am not looking for the answer to the question "Where do I belong?" For the poem gives no answers. To a certain extent it is a question, a structure unto itself, woven out of questions that have not been asked.

As I understand it, a poem is not a reaction to the world in which a human being finds himself, but to the world that he carries inside himself. I may, for example, live in Berlin. But is the place inside me Berlin? To what extent Berlin? Which Berlin? Where on earth is Berlin? Perhaps I have a Berlin inside me that is located close to the equator.

My poems are perhaps an echo of these questions. Every human being carries a map inside himself, and that is his childhood. I draw my poems on this map, with my own scale. In the process I sometimes follow paths that have been previously marked, sometimes new ones. At other times they are old tracks that have been wiped away. Until I was eight, I spent my childhood in Istanbul. I always experienced Istanbul as a city rich in history and mystery. When I was eight, I went with my family to Germany. From then on, family was for me like a window that opens onto the past. Then I grew up in Munich. There were almost no Turks in my surroundings. The Turks in Germany were completely different from those Turks in my social circle in Turkey. I first perceived Germany as a book. An alphabet that smells good and delights in colors. The book that taught me German. Later I read Kafka, Bachmann, Rilke, and Trakl in high school.[2] At the time Germany appeared to me more as a language than as a land. To date, nothing about that has changed.

GÖKHAN: *Ritual der Jugend* [Ritual of youth, 1987] is your first book to have been published in Turkish [1994]. How does it feel to be a Turkish poet?

ŞENOCAK: Writing poems in German does not mean that one is a German. The fact is, though, that my generation, which has grown up in Germany, is now a part of Germany. Against the background of my own biography it seems completely natural to me as a Turk to be a German citizen and to write poems in German. I know that the people around me think differently about that. The change that Turks in Germany are undergoing sparks reactions, not only among the Germans, but also among the Turks. Germany today tends more toward provincialism than universalism. Reunification also entailed a fencing off against the outside. The insistence on one-dimensional identities stands in opposition to multiculturalism.

I don't know whether the translation of my poems into Turkish can resolve this tension (*diese Spannung aufheben*). This book has brought me closer to Turkish poetry, which means a very great deal to me. And I have the language of my translator to thank for that.

GÖKHAN: Yüksel Özoğuz, who translated your poems into Turkish, wrote in an essay that your real identity expresses itself in your poems, in the poetic mode, and in your fiction. In your essay "Tradition and Taboo" you put it this way: "The identified stranger loses all intimacy. Everything must be revealed."[3] Another interesting title from one of your essays asks, "When Is the Stranger at Home?"[4] Is your poetry compensation for your being a stranger, or is the reverse the case?

ŞENOCAK: The answer to this question is connected to my reply to your initial question. The concept of what is strange is so laden with literary associations that it can scarcely be understood and captured by daily language usage anymore. Just think of all the things you allude to when you say, "I am a stranger" (*Ich bin ein Fremder*), or, "He is a strange man" (*Er ist ein fremder Mann*). Aside from the "stranger" who recalls the works of Kafka and Camus, there is also the "stranger" in our mystic tradition.[5] Someone who reads my biography can look for these traces in my poetry. For me, metaphors are junctures that the subject (*Subjekt*) creates in language. In lyric poetry there lies hidden, not the voice of an abstract society, but the voice of an individual. Metaphors are the subject's points of linkage (*Verknüpfungspunkte*) in language.

GÖKHAN: In *Ritual der Jugend* there are places where one can observe a patient quest for home (*Heimat*), as for example in the following lines: "a closet without light / shall I call home / a wooden horse/shall I erect in me" [*einen Schrank ohne Licht / soll ich Heimat nennen / ein hölzernes Pferd / in mir aufstellen*]; "To whom does this land belong in winter" [*Wem gehört dieses Land im Winter*]. There is also yet another level of perception that manifests itself in terms such as "house," "door," "room," and "window" (all objects that concern space). In my opinion the terms that stand out on both levels are "home" and "house." Who knows, maybe this impression results from a preconceived notion of a Turkish poet who writes in German. The house is a temple—do you believe that the quest for home represents a form of idolatry (*Anbetung*)?

ŞENOCAK: You can ask this question in good conscience. Even in the poetry of an author who writes in Turkish, the term "house" can carry a meaning. As, for example, with Behçet Necatigil.[6] What interests me is when a house becomes one's own house for a human being. By the way, I do not use the terms "home" and "house" in the figurative sense. What interests me are the feelings that are entailed when one settles down in one place. For example, the relationship between hotel and house. Your house can be in your home, but it may be that your house is not your home (*Heimat*). Or you are at home (*in der Heimat*), but it is not your house. My poetry is determined by the harmony or dissonance that the individual feels with his surroundings. At this point I must mention that the poems in *Ritual der Jugend* were written in the years 1984 to 1986. This time span followed the years 1980 to 1984, during which my contact with Turkey was reduced to a minimum. My turning to Turkey anew after 1984, however, brought new distances, new approaches, new influences and reactions in tow. That was just the time when I was translating the poems of Yunus Emre. Moreover, I also translated some poems into German by the Turkish folk song poets Pir Sultan Abdal, Kaygusuz Abdal, and Karacaoğlan.[7]

For a while one used to say that poets of foreign nationality who wrote in German in Germany were "observing Germany from the outside and holding up a mirror to it." Actually, it's rather the case that we hold up a mirror from the outside to the home that we have left.

October 1994

Interview, conducted in German by Karin Yeşilada
for the Berlin Tagesspiegel *(1995)*

May One Compare Turks and Jews, Mr. Şenocak?

TAGESSPIEGEL: What do all the commemorative events of this year mean to you as a Turkish author in Germany?

ŞENOCAK: One can immigrate to a country, but not to its past. In Germany, history is read as a diary of the "community of fate" (*Schicksalsgemeinschaft*), the nation's personal experience, to which Others have no access.[1] This conception of history as ethnic, collective memory was tied to the question of guilt after the crimes of the Nazis. In the meantime, the many pages of the diary have turned into commemorative plaques, before which one stands reverently on anniversaries. Yet history also plays a key role in the question of whether a country is open for immigrants. Can immigrants participate in shaping the German future without having access to a shared history with the native population? Is it possible to weld peoples with different histories together into one nation? For the Germans the dissolution of the ethnically defined concept of history could lift the burden of their historically rather negative self-perception. That would be important for the peaceful development of the nation-state in Germany.

TAGESSPIEGEL: Haven't recent events also placed Mölln and Solingen on the commemorative plaques of German history?

ŞENOCAK: History is, to be sure, not only the past. It also represents continuity. Does the labor of remembrance recognize this at all? I have the feeling that this so-called overcoming (*Bewältigung*: here, of the past) in this place is intended to package history, as one packs up things or buildings: in commemorative speeches, in commemorative plaques, in rituals.[2] It is time for us to unpack German history, for us to see causes and consequences. Only then will we understand what resistance there is in Germany today toward immigrants.

53

TAGESSPIEGEL: Do you see parallels between the history of Jews and the history of Turks as minorities?

ŞENOCAK: After the emancipation of the Jews in the nineteenth century, and even at the beginning of the twentieth century, questions arose that must likewise be asked today, in a time warp, about the Turks in Germany. A society dominated by a social majority regards the "Others" as foreign (*Fremde*), as not belonging. Above all, religion marks a line of separation. To be sure, the Jews asked themselves these questions against the backdrop of over a thousand years of history in Germany. The Turks raise these questions after thirty years in Germany. The minority must discuss whether it wants assimilation or not. The Turks are doing this now very passively, in code, virtually under the table. But as the third generation comes of age, that is to say, in the next ten years, these questions will be on the table openly, for Germans and for Turks.

TAGESSPIEGEL: The thirty-year history of migration is compounded by a story that has been passed down for centuries about the "Turkish Peril" to Europe. Today one speaks of the Islamic threat. Where do you locate the position of the Turkish "intellectual"?

ŞENOCAK: Precisely there where all these thought patterns and clichés come together. With its cultural history of the last two centuries, Turkey is a battlefield of ideas about progress, about Enlightenment, and about resistance to these ideas. A new approach to identity grows out of this resistance, one that is no longer merely regressive but also active. In Europe one fails to notice this. One can tell by looking at the ideas of young thinkers in Turkey who adhere to the Islamic tradition that they are ceasing to react to things European and trying to find their own path to the present. (I don't say to modernity, because they are very critical of modernity.) The fault line between European Enlightenment and the "Orient" belongs to a single society—to one mode of thought, which developed around the Mediterranean over twenty centuries as the legacy of monotheistic religions and Greek philosophy. The Mediterranean is a cradle of ideas. We will see that the center of things European lies not in Bonn or London but in Jerusalem, in Tunis, in Rome, in Istanbul. Centers that occupy our thoughts today, for reasons pertaining to economic and political power, have to be evaluated culturally in a completely different way. This will come to the surface more and more as conflicts between the European and the Islamic world unfold. Europe needs a concept for its relationships to the Mediterranean region. Intellectuals in Turkey, but also in the Balkans, for example, in Sarajevo, have cultivated a tradition of mediation.

TAGESSPIEGEL: Are "German Turks" cosmopolitan citizens of the world, or do they rather resemble Moorish Spaniards?

ŞENOCAK: Neither one nor the other! In the first generation German Turks were Anatolian farmers who were catapulted with the speed of light into the late industrial culture of German metropoles. They incurred much damage in the process, at least concerning their health. In the second generation they are already citizens of German cities who commute back and forth a lot. The third generation, especially in Berlin, will be residents of the metropolis. This generation will come closest to the image of the cosmopolitan. On the one hand, they will be well adapted because they have to change inherited traditions and climb the economic and political ladder. At the same time, there are indications that they will continue to be regarded as foreign. These indications also come to light as the door to German history is unlocked (*Entschlüsselung*). This is the Jewish experience that is passed on to us. I have to phrase it so pessimistically because I see no indications of change. That would be possible only if society took leave of its genealogical model, which defined German belonging in ethnic terms, only if society accepted instead an open, heterogeneous idea of a nation-state, as is common in Western states. In that case the immigrant's stance toward the state, toward its constitution, and toward its politics would be at issue. Germany is far removed from this approach. The minorities remain foreign, in spite of their adaptation. This will cause tension, which will in turn look familiar to us from history. The history of Jews in Germany and their assimilation is accompanied by a tense debate, which was especially sparked by Zionism and its thesis that there is no German-Jewish cultural symbiosis.[3] This thesis posits that mediation failed, that the

Jew remains Jew and the German—who defines himself as non-Jew—remains German. Today's picture reveals that many Turks in Germany perceive themselves as a lobby for Turkey because they, on the one hand, cover their backs in order to have a place to flee in case they are threatened. But at the same time they want to have an active life in Germany. Yet even if they have assimilated, they are very far from being regarded as inconspicuous citizens.

TAGESSPIEGEL: The failure of a German-Jewish symbiosis is superseded today in political figures such as Ignatz Bubis or Michel Friedman.[4] A new figure of the German Jew emerges there. In the figure of the German-Turkish intellectual I see a similar possibility for synthesis. At the same time, Turkey's perspective is oriented "with a broken gaze toward the West," as the title of one of your books suggests.[5] This gaze discovers the Turkish clientele in Germany. Do you see this threatening the dialogue?

ŞENOCAK: What dialogue? There can be a dialogue between human beings, between authors, politicians, members of the clergy. But between countries? The phrase "cultural exchange" leads one to believe that one can mediate in cases of conflict. This exchange does not ensue from curiosity about the Other, but rather it follows the conflict. That leads to an interest devoid of pleasure; the erotic component is missing. The Turks feel themselves unloved, often misunderstood, badly portrayed. This feeling of cutting a bad figure unites Turks domestically and abroad. But can one improve this image when one is a citizen of a state that locks up those who think differently, a state whose prime minister has to urge that instruments of torture be removed from police stations?[6] The Turks in Europe would have to develop an independent voice vis-à-vis Turkish politics. This voice would have to be not just self-pitying but capable of self-criticism.

There is hope in the fact that, fifty years after the nearly complete annihilation of Jews in Germany, there are once more citizens of Jewish faith there. That there can be something like a Turk who is Muslim but also a German citizen. The hope that people of Italian, Greek, Turkish, and Arab descent can communicate with each other in German in Germany and are citizens, from my perspective, is still a utopia. In Germany this is portrayed as reality. But the reality was and is a strained situation. They are defined as belonging to a different type (*andersartig*), and they are made to justify the fact that they belong. Or they accept their isolation. Under certain circumstances a marginal position in society can have its charms. Assimilation or isolation, mixed identities or ghettoization, these options produce tensions. Two questions remain decisive: Will the minority that adapts be able to achieve recognition in doing so? And who wants to block this recognition?

April 1995

Thoughts on May 8, 1995

My father experienced World War II on the radio. In 1938 the wealthy people in the village had put their money together and purchased the first radio set. It was set up in the village's only coffee house. There people met and listened to the Voice of Ankara or the Voice of Bakı. In 1941 Stalin's armies stood at the Turkish border in the Caucasus. In the summer of 1941 people anticipated their invasion. The border regions were evacuated. Hitler's surprising attack on the Soviet Union prevented the Russian invasion of Turkey. Hitler was highly rated. In Turkey there was no love lost for the Soviet Union, which had attacked Finland and divided up Poland with the Germans. But the Germans had been brothers in arms in World War I. They were remembered well and gladly. They were even admired for their fastidiously proper behavior and their organizational talent.

In World War I my grandfather was on the Turkish-Russian front. He and his father were taken prisoner in 1916. Both of them survived the imprisonment. The czar's empire collapsed. A new world arose on Russian soil. Whoever sympathized with this new world was considered in Turkey as godless. Although even modern Turkey was a godless republic, it persecuted these godless others (*diese Gottlosen*).[1] Turkey was spared in World War II. My father, who was born in 1926, belongs to this fortunate generation, which had no active experience with war.

What access does someone whose father experienced World War II on the radio, far from the battlefields, have to this event? My father was rendered an uninvolved witness by virtue of that new technology for disseminating news. Meanwhile we have all become uninvolved witnesses of one war or another, wars that take place at a greater or lesser distance from our houses.

In 1945 my father experienced neither a liberation nor a collapse.

He was neither victim nor perpetrator. This vantage point allows me to raise a few questions.

Without a doubt all those peoples who were occupied, persecuted, and subjugated by Nazi Germany were liberated in 1945. But what happened in Germany? Was only a regime defeated in Germany or an entire people that had actively or passively made itself complicitous? That this Germany was allowed to come back into existence after all the crimes to which it had given rise strikes me as a hugely civilizing accomplishment on the part of the Allied powers. Their prescription was not revenge, the total annihilation of the enemy, but rather curing him with pragmatic means. The division of Germany was no means to a cure, but presumably a calculated side effect. Yet after the collapse of the "Third Reich" Germany was divided not only into East and West but also into victims and perpetrators.

The victims were held in memory. One would have most preferred to forget the perpetrators overnight. The more one concerned oneself with the victims, the more one succeeded in forgetting the perpetrators. For the preoccupation with the victims led above all to attention being distracted away from the perpetrators. The burden of memory was laid on the shoulders of the victims. Sometimes the symbolic rituals that revolve around the victims even have something obscene to them. They have an effect like gestures of memory—as though one were extending to the victims in retrospect a right to their pain. In Germany one calls the cult that revolves around the victims "mastering the past" (*Vergangenheitsbewältigung*). A nebulous concept. For can a people liberate itself from its own history in the same way in which it can liberate itself from oppression and foreign rule?

How do Germans deal with their difficult history? Not the fiftieth anniversary of the war's end on May 8, but the overcoming of the German division in 1989/1990 has stirred up questions about this. Even in the years to come these questions will be debated with renewed vigor.

In sovereign, reunified Germany one no longer turns to one's own history with psychotherapeutic intentions. Word of normalcy is

59

making the rounds. History again becomes an instrument of power politics and attains its original significance for the future of the nation. The condition of the nation becomes all the more important. No longer does the nation lie half anesthetized on its sickbed, hoping for recovery. The patient assumes that he has been successfully cured and is free to go out. One knows how newly recovered patients can be. They are especially inclined to cast warnings about their still labile condition into the wind. Only with time can one tell if pathogenic sources are still latent in their bodies and could lead to relapses. Today Germany finds itself in such a difficult transition.

The period from 1933 to 1945 remains a wound in German memory. Has the wound scarred over? Are charlatans being allowed to treat the wound, which has long been under lock and key, with their questionable salves? The collapse of Germany as a nation defined by culture (*Kulturnation*) ended in 1945, but it began with Hitler's seizure of power in 1933.[2] Is there really a consensus about this in this country?

Germany lost World War II in 1945. The Nazi regime was defeated. On the other hand, the subtle consequences of National Socialism continue to affect Germany even today. Does the Nazis' brutal effort to render Germany ethnically homogeneous have nothing to do with the present resistance to acknowledging, in Germany in 1995, the ethnic diversity that has arisen through migration?

History is far too seldom confronted with the present. Remembrance then becomes above all a symbolic act. Through remembering one imagines that one could make restitution (*Wiedergutmachung*).[3] The achievement of remembrance is presented to the victims as a calculation. Remembering the victims is absolutely necessary. But what were and are the consequences of this remembering? It is well known that the Federal Republic of Germany was not an uncomfortable place for many former Nazis. Many of them were able to continue their careers after a brief reorientation. United Germany is that country in which four thousand to five thousand attacks and transgressions against "foreigners" (*Fremde*) take place annually. The foreigners in Germany, most of whom have been at home here for a long time, barely bother to reflect on the history of the Germans.

Now, when one often speaks of the new world order, it seems appropriate to look more closely at the old world order. Otherwise danger threatens. This danger would arise if what is new proved to be a bad surprise, that is, the return of the old, of that which has failed, of that which is condemned again and again to fail.

In Germany fifty years after the war's end, paths of remembrance must be sought that lead into the present. There must be something else on these paths other than mute monuments and ceremonious speeches held in a solemn voice.

May 1995

Between Orient and Occident

Faith and law are not my concern. There is an I deeper inside me.—
Yunus Emre, *Das Kummerrad/Dertli Dolap* [The wheel of woe],
translated by Zafer Şenocak

It is no coincidence that it was not a tome of scholarship but a work
of fiction such as *The Satanic Verses* that provoked the "engineers of
faith" in the Islamic world.[1] For as a word magician, Salman Rushdie
occupies the place abandoned by religion. Even more than this, he
reveals the emptiness of this place. Poets compete with the prophets;
the Qur'an already tells us that. Poets and prophets recover words
from a hidden language.

Rational cognition and secularization everywhere transformed
human perception of the world in fundamental ways. Yet, unlike the
West, the Islamic world lost its mythic foundations with moderniza-
tion. It was not transformation that determined progress, but a radical break with tradition. A crude rationalism proclaimed that almost
the entire history of ideas that had gone before was superstition.
What remained were rationalist and dogmatically religious (*integristisch*) zealots. Some of them make a religion out of science; the
others make a science out of the "last, perfect revelation."[2]

Rather than penetrating into the deeper layers of their own soil,
people wanted to cement over the muddy ground in order to move
forward more quickly on it. Under the cement a repressed, multi-
layered world continues to slumber, with roots in all kinds of different systems of thought and views on life. This world is peopled
with mystics like Yunus Emre, lawless men like Pir Sultan Abdal,
skeptics like Ibn Rushd, erotomaniacs like Omar Khayyam, possessed
men like Mansur.[3] Islamic culture is heterogeneous and cannot be
grasped with the West's customary concept of Islam. In public con-

sciousness and in the media this concept has more and more de-
volved into a slogan for that which is strangely foreign, threatening,
and archaic.

Understood superficially, Islam is above all a way of life, a mode of
communication, a way of gazing from one's Self to the Other. In the
process Islam orders the world according to polarities. Faith opposes
lack of faith, calm and order oppose unrest and chaos, what is permitted opposes what is forbidden.

This dichotomous view of the world is in no way archaic; rather, it
is thoroughly compatible with modernity. The civilizing idea can as
little come to fruition without its imagined opposite, the barbarian,
as the Islamic doctrine of salvation can without the world of those
who have strayed. Neither its distance nor its strange foreignness
makes the Islamic world an enemy of the West. The perception of
Islam as enemy thrives on the image's very closeness and relatedness
to the West. Whoever looks carefully recognizes elements on the
surface of Islamic culture today that have been repressed into uncon-
sciousness in the enlightened and secularized world. One sees in the
body of "Islam" what one does not want to see in oneself—above all,
sensuality and violence.

Fixing the Other as belonging to a different type is a formula
of fashionable culturalism. It hardens positions by ascribing to the
other character an inability to change. Fleeing into culturalism makes
it possible to keep the Other at a distance from oneself. These projections and patterns of repression have often been described. An
entire library could be effortlessly compiled with works on "Self and
Other" (*"Das Eigene und das Fremde"*). In the post-hermeneutic age
everything seems to have been said already about understanding the
Other. Meanwhile, all circles are united in their renunciation of
understanding.[4]

Communication between the enlightened, secularized cosmopolitan culture of the West and the various facets of the Islamic present is
threatening to fail completely. Whoever remains committed to the
Enlightenment in this seeming dead end of a conflict must ask questions, not only of the Other, but also of himself. This self-questioning

no longer takes place when "wanted" posters for the Other are broadcast into living rooms by the millions. Nowhere is the thought of Enlightenment more fragile than where quickly gained insights become certainties, where certainty begins to rule and the riddles lose significance.

Can a society survive without mythic foundations? In modernity excursions into history turn, again and again, into spooky roller coaster rides (*Geisterbahn*). In the end one aims to fight the horrific shape of the Other with violent means. Yet what happens when one leaves the tunnel behind and things do not look any different in the light than in the darkness?

It is not only in the Islamic world that the future of modernity depends on how one deals with myths. In the West, where the dialectic of Enlightenment and a critique of rationalism have long belonged to the canon of contemporary thought, such a debate is a matter of course. For Islamic cultures, on the other hand, other laws are apparently supposed to hold. There one continues to pay verbal tribute to a crude rationalism and a flattened concept of Enlightenment. One blindly clings to models of progress that have been abandoned elsewhere.[5]

There is only one way out of these contradictions today. We must risk a renaissance of universalism. Thinkers such as Feyerabend and Illich and their works have long since made their appearance in the catalogs of Muslim publishers.[6] An independent critique of Hegel is one of the most significant fields of research for young Muslim thinkers in Turkey. A critical stocktaking of the Enlightenment legacy is of fundamental importance for the continued existence of enlightenment for the world. What is missing is a history of Orient and Occident touching each other (*eine Berührungsgeschichte*), one that does not document the deeds and misdeeds of military generals, but rather one that excavates and decodes European images of Muslims and Muslim images of Europe.

Slumbering images are the most insidious. They attend our gaze, evade inspection, and distort things. Simultaneously they are often the source of artistic inspiration and a creative reordering of thought.

Repressed, violence feverishly works its way up from deeply embedded mental frameworks.

In the West the Islamic world is increasingly reduced to its inherent potential for violence. In light of the brutality of rulers and rebels in this part of the world, this is understandable. Even worse than the violence perpetrated by regimes and institutions is the absence of a fundamental critique of violence. Islamic tolerance, often invoked, has been reduced to a clever witticism at podium discussions. Yet moral indignation alone is of little help. It remains at best a well-meaning gesture that can even be transformed into a subtle form of isolation if it is coupled with the culturalization of thought patterns.

In the media reality of the late twentieth century, social processes and the movements of thought are perceived, if at all, only in the spotlight of spectacular events—calls to murder someone, for example. But the communications thicket also allows for new, crosswise connections, which raise doubt. Salman Rushdie gave rise not to insult but to uncertainty with *The Satanic Verses*. Tying diverse mythological strands together, the fictive approach to layers of Islamic mythology that have been cemented over, all this may have made the work into a dangerous, condemnable text in the eyes of those who sit on the concrete. Much too timidly, the discussion that this book actually calls for has begun in the Islamic world: What status accrues to fiction in our perception of the world? To which mythic foundations do we take recourse when we reorganize our lives today?

These questions transcend particular cultures. Opening up mono-cultural discourses could allow them to be elaborated on a more differentiated plane. Current thought patterns, which distinguish between an "enlightened" West and an "archaic" Orient and invoke the "clash of civilizations," are better suited for cartoon stencils.

May 1995

Beyond the Language of the Land

I. I have no claim to home (*Zuhause*). For I know words that I do not speak. And I speak words that I do not know.

II. The Others brace their collective identity against me. Can one lean on something that threatens to suffocate one?

III. No land is as large as language. None is so generous that one can take one's place in its language without further ado.

IV. There, where memory was and where memory was without language in fragments of dreams, structures are forming, slowly growing more distinct. Thinking becomes a house, in which people gather and join forces, and from which they sing and shoot together. Songs and salvos alternate.

V. Am I in between? Without protection? Or am I with the marksmen, sometimes here, sometimes there, changing from one house to another?

VI. To enjoy protection means to have sold one's skin. Without skin it is easier to live. But does that make one safe?

VII. When I change houses, people look at me with suspicion. The exchange of words recalls the exchange of prisoners. Am I bringing information about the enemy, or did they send me? Am I an informant or a messenger? Am I an informal collaborator (*informeller Mitarbeiter*), who is not at home in the memory of houses, who freezes in them?[1]

VIII. I sought a language and found many languages. I overheard some, forgot others, and didn't understand others in turn. I will not leave the languages as they are. I will circumscribe them. I will tell of those that have gone away, those that have remained. Those that have remained listen but understand poorly. Those that are gone no longer hear what they understand.

IX. I am not in between, for I have lost my sense of direction. Often I do not recognize the camps, have to ask my way through. Then I am found out, as someone who does not know his way. Then I am scrutinized, eyed, eavesdropped on, and suspected until I leave again.

X. I am alive because I do not remain in one place for long. This is how I elude their grasp. If they do not grasp me, I am free but lonely. Loneliness is a loud word that one says aloud only in the presence of many.

XI. One can name the houses once they have become camps. But does this act of locating help? Does it provide orientation? One could put up signs that point in the right direction. But even then it is not certain that one can read these signs, for the language of the houses is varied. At least everyone could find his own house. And if one has no house?

XII. I hear the sharpshooters every day. I can no longer tell whether they are distant or near. In the world that we inhabit, distances are without meaning. One is oneself unattainable.

XIII. I do speech exercises in order to remember. Figures surface that claim they are my father, my mother. An entire family surfaces in the imagination, persons who, despite their closeness, lose nothing of their strangeness.

XIV. I have transformed my father into a mother and her body into language. I was not able to find the word that undoes everything that has happened.

XV. When and how do speech exercises become poems? When others repeat them? When others regard themselves in them as in mirrors? How does one see oneself in a shattered mirror, also in fragments?

XVI. The Others brace their language against me. It is a perfect, locked house. Every perfect house is locked. If one had access, one would feel superfluous, or unfitting. But there is no entrance.

XVII. In the language of the Others I find letters that I remember, but they are not yet words. They are letters that, together, don't remind me of anything. Nonetheless, I put them together. A new language? My language? The letters are well known, but the words are new for me. I would like to build this language in such a way that it has windows on every side. This language makes access possible. I just don't know where.

xviii. Sometimes language appears as an abandoned house. That is a rare, happy moment. The entrance stands open. One can settle in.

xix. One will have to scrape the residue off language in order to heal the wounds of communication.

xx. My father believes. My mother nods. I doubt. But even the doubters look for someone who gives them confirmation. This person believes in turn and invites them to nod. Shaking heads and nodding tear the world into two camps. In the process those who shake their heads believe they are nodding, and those who nod believe they are shaking their heads. You can't believe it, but it can drive you to despair.

xxi. One says a wordless good-bye. One sings no songs. Language was in a greater rush to be gone.

xxii. Between doubt (*Zweifel*) and despair (*Verzweiflung*) lies the genuinely uncharted terrain. Nothing has been built on it. It is not dominated. No languages can be learned there, no wounds healed, no riddles solved. People meet there from all corners of the world. Just like that.

November 1995

Paul Celan

I do not want to approach Paul Celan as a scholar would.[1] I would like to comment only on the Paul Celan who has accompanied me as long as I have been writing.

In our times there can be no talk at all of attentiveness toward poetry. With this remark I do not mean to sound one of the usual laments claiming that lyric poetry is no longer read. The diminishing significance of lyric poetry is not something I would document with decreasing publication runs, but rather with our relationship to language.

Our relationship to our language is not face to face. In the beginning was the word. The act of disappearing in language has accompanied human beings forever. Conscious recognition of this disappearing in language began in Romanticism. It became a foundational experience of modernity. The path of poetry follows, with acts of resistance, the expulsion from language. What remains behind is a system of signs that makes reference to itself again and again. Its communicative qualities have been lost.

Celan is a master of disappearing, which is erroneously designated as falling silent. He who falls silent can no longer be heard. But that which has disappeared, that which cannot be said, exists. Even intensively so, in condensed form. This intensity is part of the unmistakable tone of Celan's poetry.

Since Celan, poetry has been created on the narrow ridge between the act of disappearing and the state of having disappeared. Poetry lives off the substance of language, which is under attack. Poetry is the view that language has of human beings. How much we are still able to see is not only a question of our eyesight but also a question of our language.

"Can a human being bear the truth?" This was Ingeborg Bachmann's question. Paul Celan's question is, "Can a human being bear language?"[2]

Human beings have had to bear quite a bit in this century. Especially Europe remains deeply marked by the events of two world wars and the largest genocide of all times. Writing poetry in the shadow of this time was and is not easy. It is all the more difficult to write poetry in the shadow of fading memory. History cannot be settled by human beings bit by bit. Its burden never lessens.

Paul Celan's poetry is borne by remembrance. Because it bears so much, its voice is not unbearably ceremonious.

Language never expresses mere naked existence. Where it has not been used up, it is remembrance. Celan's entire oeuvre serves as a legacy of linguistic (im)possibilities.

What does the daily life of someone without place look like? Many contemporaries have made this question the basis of their poetic creativity. With Celan, on the other hand, placelessness is not lived. It describes the state of life itself.

The poet, who resides within the word, leaves the land. Rarely was Celan at the place where his words were born. His words were far away from their roots. German is a language, but what is Germany? A land without its language? For Celan, German is a language, his language without land.

Whoever is at home does not think; whoever thinks is not at home. Human beings cast no shadow beyond language, beyond this tangle of roots. He who is bound to language is the most firmly rooted of all on shaky ground.

When I began to write, my world shrank down to a few words. I had no history of my own in the language in which I wrote. So I had to construct my own dictionary for myself. I picked up the words where I found them and led them to the place where I was. And sometimes, more seldom, the words came to get me, led me into their land.

Every language begins and ends within an individual (*in einem selbst*). The roots cannot be traced. One's own dictionary is sealed.

Fine differences sometimes yield crude similarities. Sometimes a sense of being neighbors, standing next to each other, grows out of what is similar. But at other times, what is similar increases the distance. Neighborhoods do not necessarily suggest similarity. Jewish/German, Muslim/German, Hebrew/German, Turkish/German, how much proximity can a language bear? How much neighborhood, how much interference? When poetic language can be reconciled with something, it has betrayed itself to its meaning. Celan's language bore little reconciliation.

Language is the irreconcilable landscape. One puts no roots down there. In language one enters a path. One marvels at the blossoms on the roots that have been hacked off. Celan's hacked-off roots touched my hacked-off roots. An oddly distinct sound. Poets are not mediators but mixers. They blur the lines on the blackboards of memory. These become visible only in the absence of order. Under the maps, timetables, and other organizational aids there are hints that, on occasion, make our stance less certain. Often, though, they deepen our access.

The mystics in the background call out. The Kabbalah and Sufism, the proximity (*Nachbarschaft*) of a region, yesterday's voice in various languages.[3] Something always remains in our ear. A residue of sound.

Whoever plays with his hacked-off roots places himself in no-man's-land; he touches a no-man's-rose as it wilts.[4] He revives places that have drifted away and are nowhere to be found (*verschollen*). I followed Celan's tracks and ended there where my own roots got lost.

November 1995

The One and the Other Child

I was twice a child.[1] Once in Turkish, once in German. As a Turkish child I could not speak any German; as a German child I could already speak Turkish. Thus the Turkish child learned German. But the German child never had to learn Turkish.

Whenever there is talk of my childhood, I never know exactly which one is meant, the Turkish one or the German one. If I see a written word such as *ruh*, I first have to hear how it is pronounced in order to understand what it means. The Turkish child translates it for the German child as *ruh*, "soul," but the German child shakes his head; he knows exactly what is meant by *ruh*. After all, it simply means being quiet, having peace, hush now.

I do not want to interfere in their argument. There would be no point. Let each one believe what he wants, understand what he wants, tell what he wants. Each one in his own language.

The Turkish child is intimidated. He has met many strangers. He never became an adult. He is alive. The German child on the other hand had to think and die in order to grow up. Thus, I am now a child in Turkish and an adult in German. I can speak whatever I want, write whatever I want, in whatever language I choose; every one of my words has a Turkish childhood. When the German forgets something, the Turkish child remembers. When the Turkish child doesn't understand something, the German explains. Can this turn out well?

"The German is a stranger," my father says. "We don't understand him," my mother says. "Many things keep us apart." They cherish and protect the Turkish child, see to it that he never grows up. He is always supposed to stay the way they imagine him to be, well behaved, innocent, shy. They are afraid of the German. He is foreign to them. When he was a child, they didn't pay much attention to him. They didn't know for certain if he was their own child.

"It's me," I always say whenever I visit them. As if my appearance were not enough for them to recognize me. Yes, it's still me. "We haven't lost you, boy, you're back," my mother calls out. My father sings. I could understand everything, have the feeling of being home. But I only nod fleetingly, like someone who wants to indicate that he has little time and cannot stay.

I would like to question my parents about my German childhood. But they remember only the Turkish child. In their eyes I am only the one child. My German "I" responds calmly. It leaves the Turkish child in peace. The Turkish child turned eight years old. Then he became immortal. He has conversations with himself. Sometimes he also writes letters to old acquaintances. Letters that he cannot send, because he doesn't know what has become of the addressees.

Territories

I

In Germany some things are important: the tree of genealogy, the tribe and the tree, and the table for regulars, the regulars and the table.[1]

Thus it happened that I burrowed into my own trunk without happening upon a tree or even a table. Instead there were only loose leaves to be found inside, leaves that could no longer be unequivocally assigned to any tree, crossings that the wind had designed, with stubbornly independent patterns, sometimes not to be identified. And a table? Where did people sit in our tribe, where did they write, where did they change the world? In the wake of long investigations I stumbled across an astonishingly simple solution to this complicated question. On the ground. Where else?

Our tribe ate the leaves up off the ground, crossed them with the leaves of other tribes, which the wind had borne to us depending on which way it was blowing, sometimes from the north, sometimes from the south, sometimes from the east, sometimes from the west. In this manner our tribe had missed out on the development of the table, which one should have set up in the middle of everything in order to become definitively settled, in order really to stem from the ground on which we ate. In my research I have also sensed that my tribe tends to lose that which is most important, that is, its grounding. Instead it sets out on the path that leads to other tribes, which—all in possession of their well-developed genealogical trees—desire only a few fresh leaves for themselves. To this end they printed special forms. But were our leaves fresh enough? Or had they perhaps been on the road too long to turn green again somewhere else on a strange trunk?

II

My father sits on a tree stump, the roots of which are identical with the bones of my grandfather. That is how far back he went. What

74

grounds me? I have planted a loose collection of leaves. Turned many colors, sometimes lighter, sometimes darker. Spoken little, written little, only my name when I had to. I didn't have much more.

Then someone came who was passing through and took everything with him. Was it a stranger? Was it my brother?

I stood for a while with him by the side of the road. A third person could scarcely tell if he had come or I had come, if he would go or I would. In the end we exchanged no addresses. He had none, and mine was known to him.

III

People are curious to know where I come from. Few are interested in the path that I have taken. Everyone is obliged to take the shortest route home. Paths create fear. Detours give rise to suspicions. En route people cannot be identified. Is someone a harmless traveler with a set destination or a highway robber? Does someone have a passport, a visa, the right color of skin, a suitable face? Detours must be avoided at all cost. If they cannot be avoided, they must be shortened. Only a certain point at the end of the road creates security. One is not well cared for there, but secure. At such a point one can establish a firm place for oneself (*sich festorten*), orientation.

IV

Since I have become a stranger, I have faith again. The stranger always has his God with him. The stranger's God is a pocket god. Don't ask me how someone turns into this, a stranger. It must have happened in a moment when I wasn't paying attention. I did not know it from one moment to the next. No incubation period, no preparation, no test, really nothing at all. Someone speaks to you on the street, and you know it. As if that weren't enough, you believe in it too. At home, at some point, your faith becomes superfluous. You know every corner and can no longer imagine anything hidden at all. Into the dubious place of faith steps shrill certainty. There is scarcely any reason to live one's faith anymore. One reads the letters that one can, puts them together into words that one knows, and believes that one understands, thereby, all the languages of the world. As a stranger one no longer understands one's own language. One has only one's faith left.

v

We leap from one point to the other and barely know anymore where the border runs. We arrive at border stations that have been abandoned. We cannot locate them on any map. The former border runs right through us. Whoever looks inside himself stumbles upon an invisible wall. Soldiers chew on their now useless machine gun bullets. They no longer look dangerous, but can they be trusted? We must overcome our own inhibitions in order to get past the border. It is possible, but only on hidden byways.

April 1996

Which Myth Writes Me?

Whoever writes fiction is subjected to questions about the sources for his writing. The place where literature comes into being is not the writing workshop, where literature is merely articulated in language and given shape. Fictions cannot be traced to words, but to fore-words. These fore-words come out of the author's personal background, from his writing myth. This myth usually derives from a childhood experience, a pivotal experience. People often interpret literature through the author's biography. In the case of authors who live outside their native linguistic geography, questions about belonging threaten to obscure other biographical details. The mythic foundations of their work disappear completely from view.

Peter Weiss called his form of writing an "autobiographical fiction."[1] My literature, too, arises in a field of tension between personal experience and linguistic imagination. The way in which the world of experience intersects with the imaginative powers of language yields the style and form of my literary production.

On the basis of my heritage I am a member of an ethnic minority in Germany. This group is the largest minority living in Germany today—the Turks. Am I therefore a Turkish author? I write my texts primarily in German, a language that I learned when I was eight. Am I therefore a German-speaking author? Perhaps a German-speaking author of Turkish descent? Am I something that cannot, must not be? I did not ask myself any of these questions when I began to write.

Writing is something that takes you by surprise. It is an unexpected, startling act. Preparatory and practice steps in the dance take place in secret. No one can tell by looking at you that you are an author. But presumably one could always tell by looking at me that I was a Turk. That writing literature and being Turkish are directly related is a lesson that I would have to learn. Would you have written if you had not come to Germany? I never suspected discrimination behind this hypothetical question, which I always answered in the affirmative. Until one day someone asked me if there was a noteworthy literature in Turkey.

So people ask all kinds of questions. Is one asked such questions as an author or as a Turk in Germany? If one publishes a book in German as a Turk, is one then read as a German-speaking author or as a writing Turk? When the Turks in Germany began to write and did so in German, the Germans were quite surprised. After all, the formal agreements regulating the recruitment of foreign laborers had not said anything about literature. For this reason Germans are still surprised today when they encounter the phenomenon of a Turk writing in German. As we all know, surprise can impede perception. It forces us to bridge moments of paralysis, of speechlessness, of the inability to think and act, with conventional questions. Where did you learn German? How long have you been in Germany? Do you also write in Turkish? Do you intend to return? One does not read an author's texts, but rather, the biography written onto his body. Genealogy substitutes for biography. The body of the text—with its own patterns, its own concealed fore-words—disappears behind the image of the author. What motivates this type of reading? Fear of wonder? Fear of understanding or not understanding, a sense of strangeness, real or imagined?

Doesn't a sense of wonder precede every aesthetic pleasure?

Many people who come to hear my texts ask me about biographical details. But it hardly ever happens that someone asks me about the mythic foundation of my work. Scholarly commentaries often link me with authors with whom I share only the biographical detail of not being German in Germany.

Yet fiction is not reproducible. It is a unique, personal expression of linguistic consciousness. An experiential foundation in the deep structure of human consciousness. Fiction corresponds to the mythic foundation that first makes the writer into what he is, namely, an unmistakable interpreter of his world and time.

What, then, is the mythic material that informs my writing? Which myth writes me? The following remarks will not, I think, reveal anything that cannot also be found in my poetry and my prose. Many of my readers rely on my essays like crutches on which to balance their movements through the fields of my labor. But what is expressed in the essays is merely the externalized side of my literature. In lyric poetry and prose we find the paths that lead us inside. My writing myth, which winds through almost all my books, is fed by an ambivalence that I sensed in my immediate environment even as a child. This was the ambivalence between a rational and a mystical (or in more modern terms, a mysterious) experience of the world, between physics and metaphysics. Born in a country torn apart, the world experience of which was revolutionized within a single generation, into a family standing between tradition and modernity, I experienced the falsity of simple polarities at a very early age.[2] Between tradition and modernity, between rationality and irrationality there was no place of synthesis. Rather, these seeming opposites functioned like corrective mirrors when confronted with each other. The tolerance of mysticism and the uniformed violence of modernity, the open play of rational cognition and the strict, closed thought patterns of dogmatism— these were not opposites absolute unto themselves. Instead, they were defunct markers on a field of rubble, on which every element called for autonomy and yet everything was untransparently linked to everything else. My writing myth arose on this field of rubble, which seems to me to be a playground of endless possibilities.

The writer is related to the archaeologist. He is the archaeologist of his own playing field (*Spielwiese*). It may be that he stumbles onto stones that no longer fit into any architectural structure. Then he realizes that he not only reconstructs buildings but also designs them anew. The material in the field inspires, challenges, drives one to despair. In a time when dichotomous perception between cultures is fashionable, archetypal conflicts between Orient and Occident, between religions, are revived. But from my perspective an author does not stand between these things. Within himself he carries instead all the signs with which he has come into contact.

In my case I touch Anatolian-Islamic culture with its particular intersections, the Levantine culture of Istanbul, German writers who touched something different from what I touched, something that made them nonidentical with the German language in which they wrote—that is to say, above all, Jewish writers of the German language: Kafka, Benjamin, Scholem, Celan. In the case of all these writers, their writing myth is closely tied to religious tradition, especially to its mystical interpretation.[3]

I learned to distinguish a cold language from a warm one. Cold language made me rely on the formulation of certainties, on reason and its capacity for comprehension, on mathematical precision. Warm language led me, on the other hand, to the flow of language, to metaphors with their bright and dark sides, to multivalence and the indeterminate connection between mysticism and reason. My father introduced me to mystical texts. He occupied the realm of faith in my world. A man who spent his entire life waging battle against modernity with his faith, and yet completely different from the zealots who regard only their own world as valid. My mother represented mathematics. She believes only in what she can count. Nonetheless, my father's language was cold, my mother's warm. Once again a polarity thought to be fixed, a dichotomous structure, collapsed. If I attributed eros to mysticism, as was expected, it disappeared in the language, grown cold, of old texts. If I entrusted eros to womanly warmth, its language became unintelligible.

My writing myth was born. It arose at the rupture between reason and mysticism, at the main train station of eros, where coming and going is life's elixir for all those who have long since ceased to wait for angels to arrive.

Of course, not only genealogical and biographical coordinates are responsible for an author's writing myth. Was it coincidence that I distanced myself in the early 1980s from the techniques of the poetry of the everyday that determined poetic modes of writing in Germany at that time? I felt drawn to the poets of the 1950s, to [Günter] Eich, [Ingeborg] Bachmann, [Peter] Huchel, [Paul] Celan. My poetry was rich in metaphors; I rejected the maxims of prudish German epigrammatic poetry. The expressive voice with which I began to write was influenced by many things: nature, the animal world, and a turn to the myths of everyday life, myths that proliferate on the mountains of trash produced by our civilization; the perception of rifts in late modernity, the cracks in twentieth-century civilization, the metropoles with their odd moods of departure and farewell.

The turn to metaphor suggests more than a stylistic peculiarity. Metaphor is the kernel of every metaphysical experience, which exceeds rational cognition. It is the only secret left to us in a world of discoveries. Our secularized world, ruled by rationality, reacts with panic to mysteries. They are treated like relics from the past. Despite modernity's discomfort with secrets, modernity has neither been able to eliminate them, nor has it replaced them with anything else. Metaphor thus functions like a disturbance, an unsettled place in language. Rational, linear thought cannot decipher it.

The 1980s brought a heightened concern with history, above all, with those phases that had been displaced by the Enlightenment, such as the Middle Ages. Mystical traditions reasserted themselves, inscribed themselves into memory. The concept of gnosis resurfaced from the depths of seminars on religious history. Discontent with Enlightenment perspectives spread throughout the humanities. One epochal designation stood in for all these phenomena: postmodernism. Beyond such cataloging concepts as modernism and postmodernism, which may be less relevant for a writer than they are for scholars, I recognize a genie of our time that has long since escaped its bottle. We perceive our time as memory, less as memory of the past than as a memory of the present. We are fundamentally skeptical of the means and methods of perception in modernity. This skepticism unsettles our stance in the present, calls for foundations, which are then cobbled together from diverse times and places. Our world has transformed itself into a construction site. But construction does not proceed there according to a particular plan.

Not a bad time for authors, in my opinion. They are challenged to create new designs, which should be judged less in terms of normative validity than in terms of imaginative achievement.

When the basic values of modernity and Enlightenment are

shaken, then this turbulence affects communicative models for understanding between cultures. One of the basic values of the Enlightenment was its faith in the possibility of human communication. In the age of multimedial communication the concept of understanding is reconfigured. Hermeneutic models are considered more from the vantage point of the failure, not the success, of understanding. Something like a negative hermeneutic emerges, which critically interrogates what is presumed to be understood. This negative hermeneutic focuses attention instead on what has not been understood, what has been displaced and repressed.

Our world is not marked by a chasm, but by many visible and invisible fissures that simultaneously divide us and link us together.

April 1996

Translated by Martin Chalmers and Leslie A. Adelson

War and Peace in Modernity

REFLECTIONS ON
THE GERMAN-TURKISH FUTURE
(1994/1998)

Our perception is determined by two perspectives, which order our thoughts, our judgments, and our behavior.[1] First, how do we see the Other? Second, how do we see ourselves?

From the vantage point of our Western civilization, the nineteenth century was dominated by the first perspective. The whole world lay spread out before us like a map. Our finger led us to the remotest regions. Our gaze came to rest on the Other. We expanded and colonized. The nineteenth century was the high point of a civilization that had successfully turned the fruits of the Enlightenment, as well as of a social and political transformation, into technological and military superiority.

In the twentieth century, global wars for economic advantage and the subsequent conflict of ideologies superseded colonialism. The perspective, however, remained fixed on the Other, only this time it was the ideological enemy. Alliances were justified neither historically nor culturally but by a shared view of the Other, the common enemy.

After the upheavals in the communist states and the end of the Cold War, the mood in the West was then, for a short time, dominated by positive expectations, especially in Europe. Even in Germany, which is well known as a cradle of pessimism, there was evident, at least for a few months after the fall of the Berlin Wall, something like the feeling of a new beginning. After all, the division of Germany was over and, forty-five years after the end of World War II, Germany was a sovereign state once more.

Yet, as everyone knows, in the meantime the mood has veered

round completely. Instead of a more peaceful, less tense world, we have one that is constantly on the alert; instead of a new world order, there are disintegrating states, countless civil wars, ever more trouble spots. In the middle of Europe, in the territory of former Yugoslavia, a bloody war has raged for years.

After the end of the Cold War and the disappearance of the common enemy, the perspective that determined perceptions also changed. Never has Rudyard Kipling's pronouncement that "East is East, and West is West, and never the two shall meet" been more accurate than now.[2] Instead of engaging in ideological dispute with the Other, he is simply disregarded. Regard is reserved for one's own. Who are we? This question is given precedence over "Who am I?" Did postmodern theories not conjure up a dissolution of the subject? The confusion and disorientation that the individual observes in modern societies give rise to calls for principles of order that are at once new and old: nation, religion, and gender.

An idea is making the rounds: identity. It is an idea born of lack. Because what do we see when we look at ourselves? It is no longer ourselves that we see. Our self-image turns out to be a fiction. The white man's empire no longer exists anywhere. The metropoles of Western civilization, like London and Paris, which for centuries provided the whites with an illusion of homogeneity (we are by ourselves) and superiority (we are different and better), and to which the others looked with a melancholy gaze, are fallen bastions. The idea of a global civilization, dominated by the West, is not working out as planned. Westernization did not mean the simple disappearance of the other cultures.

"Those who loudly lamented the death of cultures neither wanted to know nor wanted to see that these cultures themselves, obsessed like us with the myth of affluence, have adapted to the Occidental universe, each in its own specific way. The result may be paradoxical, irrational, or like a caricature, but it attests to old customs and to the indebtedness to cultural forms, from which one derives one's own possibilities. The non-Western world is a huge quarry of forms of survival, under conditions that still have to be analyzed."[3]

As a result of the movements of migration, the non-Western today extends as far as London, Paris, or Berlin. It is just as little authentic and unspoiled as the Western. Nevertheless, the longing for authenticity is alive in it too. Origins are often nostalgically distorted. Thus ghettos come into being, in which the marginal continues to exist, and center and periphery confront one another unreconciled. They demonize the Other in themselves and themselves in the Other. It is the paradoxical, caricature-like "irrational" that allows a body of work such as that of Salman Rushdie to come into being in London. This world is threatening to anyone who wants to draw a line between himself and the Other. Because everywhere he expects to encounter the different, the Other, he also finds his own world. Wherever his gaze is directed at his own, it also discovers the Other. The gaze at one's own is disturbed. What consequences does that have for a time in which perception is, in the first instance, determined by a perspective on one's own? Resentment, bewilderment, disorientation, aggression? Is there a fortress into which one can withdraw, where the Other, even if not far away, is at least not noticeable? Where the gaze falls undisturbed upon one's own? At such times there is a longing for unity and homogeneity. The identical becomes sought after. The concept of identity finds favor. The longing for identity is by no means a concern of the mob. Identity is a highly artificial concept, which is crafted in philosophers' studies, assembled by political rulers, inhabited by the people (*Volk*), and erected on battlefields, in order to create homogeneity synthetically, an order founded on purging the Other, on annihilation of differences.

Looked at in this way, the political events of recent years are no mere accumulation of coincidence. The conflict in Bosnia is a paradigm of a global, or at least a European, conflict. Identity, homogeneity, and unity are demanded by force. Ethnic and religious boundaries turn out to be lines of separation.

In summer 1993 Professor Samuel P. Huntington of Harvard University published his thesis on a global "clash of civilizations" in the journal *Foreign Affairs* [vol. 72.3, pp. 23–49]. By this account, cultural differences between civilizations rather than ideological and economic interests would be the mobilizing forces of future world conflicts. The "fault lines" between civilizations are the front lines of the future. Huntington believes that his arguments are largely confirmed by conflicts already going on at present. The war in Yugoslavia broke out over a historically consolidated dividing line between civilizations. Additional conflicts in the Caucasus and in the south of the former Soviet Union are developing along such dividing lines. Everything points to a major clash between Western civilizations based on "Judeo-Christian" values, as Bernard Lewis puts it, and the civilizations of the East, which are shaped by Islam and Confucianism. At this point one cannot help asking the following question: Which civilization do the Chetniks [Serbian guerilla soldiers], who massacre the Muslim Bosnians in the name of Christian Europe and as successors to the Crusaders, represent? Huntington has taken care of that problem. When the aim is to homogenize Western civilization, then not only are the Muslims excluded, but the Orthodox Christians also apparently belong to a quite different tradition, which is dominated by Russia and has still to be won over for the West.

Western civilization has undoubtedly created values that it puts into practice more efficiently than other civilizations. Democracy, human rights, freedom of opinion, freedom of worship, freedom of movement, and the right to own property are among them. Yet these values have to be defended not only against external enemies, the Others, but also internally against oneself. The entire Second World War was such an internal defense. It is a tragic mistake to believe that the victory over fascism in 1945 meant its disappearance from the intellectual map of European civilization. It was France, no less, that even in the 1950s and 1960s took on a senseless war in Algeria with 1.5 million dead, in order to maintain itself as the colonial power in that country. Huntington's analysis of European reality is quite unrealistic. It puts a gloss on things that warrant no gloss. Using the ambiguous concept of "civilization," it constructs unities that are fragile in the extreme. Europe at the close of the twentieth century is a very insecure, deeply divided continent, which is playing an elaborate unification game to repress its own contradictions and conflicts.

In fact, since the 1980s, at least, Europe has been arming itself for a civilizing battle against strangers. Intellectuals pave the way for such a battle. The reincarnation of national, identity-shaping thought began in France. In the movement known under the name of the Nouvelle Droite (New Right), intellectual circles were formed and publications appeared, demanding a Europe that was prepared to defend itself and draw on its own national and religious traditions. Next to Bolshevism, a second enemy had been sighted. For the third time in history, after the Arab and Turkish military invasions, Islam was again [seen as] threatening Europe's borders. Now it was Arabs and Turks once more, not with armies but with hosts of guest workers. What at first appeared to be a harmless economic phenomenon soon developed into a momentous social phenomenon. The so-called guest workers violated the rules of hospitality, settled down, improved their economic status and became immigrants.

The ideas of the Nouvelle Droite did not remain confined to France. Now that Germany has been united, it provides a suitable exercise and breeding ground for xenophobia and nationalist ideas. Germany is the European state that has stood apart from the Anglo-Saxon understanding of democracy and the French republican conception of the state; a country on which democracy was, twice in its history, imposed from outside, by victorious powers; a country that must now stand on its own two feet and has, at the same time, the most powerful economy in Europe. It is astonishing that Huntington's essay does not deal with the element of uncertainty represented by Germany. He simply overlooks this giant in the middle of Europe, which for so long had to wear shoes that were too small for it. Now that the shoes fit again, it does not quite know where its feet will carry it.

Where does Germany belong? Were forty years' membership in the Western alliance enough to democratize Germany thoroughly? What influence will Eastern Germany, which was under the rule of an authoritarian regime for forty years, exert on Germany in the future? What attitude does newly united Germany take to its National Socialist past? Many questions clamor for our attention. They have been made more urgent because of incidents that make clear how fragile and contradictory Western civilization is, at least in Germany. Violence against foreigners, against asylum seekers, against Turks already long settled in the country, the desecration of Jewish cemeteries, attacks on synagogues and mosques have become commonplace in Germany. Surveys indicate that 13 percent of Germans sympathize with an extreme right wing, and that 34 percent express understanding for the criminal acts of right-wing extremists. Anti-Semitism appears to be firmly rooted in Europe, especially in Germany. Europe is the largest grave in the history of the sorely tried Jewish people, and the modern twentieth century the age of the most nearly successful attempt to annihilate them.

It appears to me that the real clash of civilizations is being prepared in Europe. It is a conflict between the modernity that Huntington has in mind when he talks about Western civilization and the repressed part of Western civilization, the protest against modernity that again and again rises up against modernity and yet is part of it. All the values that seem to be threatened by a confusing pluralist and multicultural society play an important part in this protest: national, religious, and gendered identity.

At the beginning of 1993 the writer Botho Strauss, one of the most important contemporary German dramatists, published an essay that profoundly disturbed Left and liberal opinion. In it he wrote, "the hypocrisy of public morality that tolerated (where it did not actively promote) the ridiculing of Eros, the ridiculing of the soldier, the ridiculing of church, tradition, and authority, has no right to be surprised if, in an emergency, its words no longer have any weight. But whose hand, whose mouth, has the power and authority to save us from far worse?"[4] With this question the author, bewildered by the complexity of modernity, returns to the bosom of German tradition. The expectation of salvation from one mouth. He could, without further ado, join with those masses in Tehran who received such salvation from the mouth of an old man.[5] It is not a question of a sense of belonging to a civilization, but of one's attitude toward modernity. The critique of civilization as practiced by Botho Strauss has something of a tradition in Germany. This tradition is not the

88

preserve of loners as Strauss, in the garb of poet and visionary, would like us to believe, but one that has a social significance and also manifests itself politically. Because for Strauss, the success of modern societies is limited to economic matters; behind that, however, the complete morbidity of this system becomes visible.

Here is Botho Strauss's conclusion:

> Given the state of things, it is now dawning on some people that societies in which economism is not at the center of all activities will, in the event of a crisis, display considerable strength or even superiority owing to a regulated limitation of needs based on faith. [. . .] We are a little too smug in our warnings against the nationalist currents in the new states of Eastern Europe and Central Asia. We no longer understand that someone in Tadjikistan can see it as a political duty to preserve his language, just as we do our lakes and rivers. We no longer understand that a people can want to assert its moral law against others and is ready to make blood sacrifice for it, and in our liberal-libertarian self-absorption we consider it to be wrong and reprehensible.
>
> But conflicts are approaching that can no longer be appeased in terms of economics, in which it could turn out to be disadvantageous that the wealthy West European has, as it were, also been living morally beyond his means, since here the "feasible" was least likely to come up against any limit. It does not matter what value we place on it, it will be hard to fight against—that the old things are not simply dead and out of date, that man, the individual as much as the member of a people, does not simply exist in the here and now. There will be a war between the forces of tradition and those of constant removal, disposal, and obliteration.[6]

Botho Strauss's essay reads like a continuation of Samuel Huntington's arguments. Yet Strauss offers a far more realistic assessment of who the warring parties will be. The conflict between modernity and antimodernity is present in all civilizations, and is most pronounced where modernity is most strongly developed and has entered a profound crisis—that is, within Western civilization itself. The conflicts between Islamic cultures and Western civilization, which Huntington predicts will be the great clash of the near future, are no more than harbingers of a struggle within civilization, for it would be foolish to believe that the face of the West would not change in the course of such a collision with fundamentalist Islam. Today, France is already revoking the state of law in the struggle with Muslim fundamentalists living in that country. In Algeria, Western civilization is maintaining itself against the Islamic opponent only by getting rid of its own values such as free, independent elections and freedom of opinion.

"Are our energies exhausted?" asks the critic and philosopher George Steiner. At the close of the millennium it is, above all, the old myths of Europe that are exhausted. The myths no longer tell stories. They are quotations without the power to arouse. Media culture promotes the receptivity of the human intellect without addressing its dark presentiments and need for spirituality. Furthermore, the discourse of postmodernity, while it has not annulled the global and linear model of progress, dominant in the West since the Enlightenment, has at least put it in question. This discourse is increasingly also being taken up by Muslim intellectuals, especially in Turkey.

[. . .][7] Precisely where cultural conflicts are concerned, our language seems used up, grammar and semantics muddled, the measure of things lost. At the same time there is a demand for communication, as can be observed from ever more meetings with themes like "The Self and the Other" or "Being Different: A Human Right?" But what is the basis of such discussions about the self and the stranger, in the age of their reproducibility?[8] In Germany, until now, it has been primarily unpleasant occurrences. The authority of events determines the place, size, and character of the discussion. The reason for a discussion with Turks is that some Turks have been burned to death by German right-wing extremists and not, for example, a self-evident interest in the existence of two million Turks living in Germany. "Turks in Germany: Only Since Their Houses Are Burning Are We

Aware of Them," ran a headline in the liberal weekly *Die Zeit* after the murders in Solingen. A fashionable cultural pessimism covers up the connections between thinking and acting, and makes possible arbitrary discussions whose only purpose is their own existence.

[. . .]

But who are the Turks in Germany? Well, one can say that they are people who come from a particular country, that is, Turkey. Is this brief observation sufficient in order to talk about the Turks in Germany? Every sense of belonging is founded on an arrangement of differences. Yet once such a sense of belonging is constructed, it depends on ignoring differences. Notions of identity that deal with "the German" or "the Turk" follow this pattern.

Recently it has become fashionable to organize meetings between Germans and Turks. Germans and Turks live together in Germany. Now they are also supposed to form an intercultural study group. The very fact that such meetings between representatives of two population groups, who have been living together in the same country for more than thirty years, have to be organized—under titles like "Week of the Foreign Fellow Citizen"—is somewhat absurd. If a Turk meets a German on the street, they are at liberty to talk about the weather. But what possibilities are open to interlocutors sitting around a table, in a conversation between Germans and Turks, if they represent "the German" and "the Turk"? Is it possible to reduce conversations to external surfaces and to events? For example, how important is what is left unsaid or misunderstood in such conversations?

Culture is the category that these encounters have in common. Yet the concept of culture is deployed as a discursive expression of one's own position. Where does one stand as a German Turk within a German-Turkish dialogue? In the middle, perhaps? Or maybe even off to the side? If one presumes that identities exist in fixed, unbroken ways, then from the vantage point of a German Turk, the German-Turkish encounter becomes a nightmarish phantasm. The question—who and what is a German or a Turk—stands stubbornly and unasked in the room. To make things easier, one leaves it untouched. But then, who is talking, and with whom?

A German-Turkish conversation operates on the basis of knowledge about the other. Occasionally this knowledge is supplemented by knowledge from the other. From where, for example, does a teacher draw his knowledge when he tells his multiculturally mixed class about Turkish literature or when he speaks about Islam? In concrete contexts, such as schools or youth exchanges, culture is no longer perceived abstractly. Instead, it is experienced in connection with the life world of the participants. Knowledge from and about each other represents the foundation for the conversation in this process. This knowledge derives from three different sources: first, from acquired knowledge, such as language, information about history, statistics on social structures, and so on; second, from vague hunches, images, and inherited but no longer documented knowledge; and third, from everyday experiences.

Let me make this more concrete. A. is a teacher in a small German town. He teaches German [language and literature] and Protestant religion. In addition to German pupils there are above all Turkish pupils in his classes. A.'s knowledge about Turkish culture stems mostly from his theological training. Luther's *Table Talk* characterizes "the Turck" as a "cunning, cruel, devious, impetuous murderer. A fox in battle."[9] A. likes to read Latin American literature. He is not familiar with Turkish authors. A. is a vegetarian and especially likes to shop at the vegetable market, whose proprietor is a Turk. When A. thinks of Turks, he mostly imagines farmers. (Almost half the population in Turkey lives in the countryside.) The vegetable grocer is not only a Turk; he is also a practicing Muslim. In his store there are brochures about Islam. One of them is also in German. A. is willing to take a brochure along and then is appalled by the bad German in the brochure. In A.'s mind anything that is printed must be flawlessly phrased and printed. A. finds that Turks are sloppy. The Turkish colleague at school, who came from Ankara and is responsible for teaching Turkish pupils in their mother tongue, confirms his impression for him. Although the Turkish teacher speaks only broken German, he knowingly reports that this brochure has been composed by enemies of the Turkish state. "You mean, by fundamentalists?"

A. asks. The Turkish teacher nods. A. wants to examine the vegetable grocer more carefully. A. asks him why his wife doesn't help him with his work, as is customary in small family operations. Besides, employing family members has its tax advantages. A. thinks that the vegetable grocer prevents his wife from showing herself in public because he is a Muslim. But the grocer is a widower and has no children. A. follows Peter Scholl-Latour's reports on Islam on television. He also reads his books on the subject.[10] He is unsettled by events in the Islamic world and decides to attend a seminar that a Protestant academy is offering under the title "Strange Neighbors: Muslims among Us."

The television images of Muslims, Luther's *Heerpredigt*, the brochure of the Muslim missionaries, the vegetable grocer with fresh goods but badly written tracts: How are these things related to the everyday encounter with Turkish children in the school?[11] There lies the real challenge. Integration is not achieved when the differences of others are used to consolidate one's own image of the world. For real integration one must cultivate, in encounters with others, a sense for multiplicity and contradiction. In the process one would have to analyze sources of knowledge beyond preconceived opinions and identities. Disparate factors would have to be deciphered as a precondition for an encounter.

This tripartite source of knowledge is not rendered any clearer by the medialization and institutionalization of knowledge in the information society. On the contrary. Contexts are produced at great speed, diverse sources of information flow together and often can no longer be told apart. Especially in arenas that produce identity, such as religion or history, the linkage between rational knowledge and irrational hunches is unavoidable. Only in public discourse, however, does this exert an unholy effect, even though public discourse allegedly follows enlightened maxims and keeps silent about that which is hidden. What is unconscious is not given to ritual but is repressed. When it is hidden, it acquires a subversive character. It breaks out again in those places where society is torn. One example of this is the fury of the national, which has seized postsocialist societies and still lies ahead for Western societies in the wake of European unification.

What is desperately needed is an archaeology of our own knowledge. Working our way through the Orient-Islam complex in Europe and the Europe complex in Turkey could perhaps overcome rigid images and allow us to perceive something beyond petrified fronts.

If consciousness is human beings' waking side, then the unconscious is the sleeping, dreaming side. Modern, rational culture depends on the sleeping side's being restricted as far as possible when humans communicate. Symbols and rituals are pushed back in favor of concepts and facts. Power over concepts and facts is also power over the world. The resulting apparatus of technology and the marketplace faces a profound crisis today because it believes it can get by without the sleeping side of human beings. As the French sociologist Alain Touraine puts it in an interview with the Turkish periodical *Nokta* [Point], remote from the highways controlled by technology, ramified byways have developed on which minority ghettos are increasingly forming. Globalization along the highways stands in contrast to the ramified paths not only of ethnic and religious identities but also of subcultures that are tending to isolate themselves. The dynamic between centers and peripheries threatens to lead to military conflict that has less and less to do with economic questions and more to do with cultural belongings and identities.

Let us return to our German-Turkish table. If the people sitting there represent politics or business, one can assume a language in which the points of agreement outweigh the differences. One is on firm ground and believes it will be possible to get by with just a few facts and concepts. Knowledge about the Other is limited, at least on the German side, to a bare minimum. [. . .] The names of towns like Mölln or Solingen become symbols of inexplicable phenomena. The localization of evil is a kind of flight. In intellectual debates there stirs a discontent with culture, which suddenly swallows up the laboriously constructed card houses of intercultural communication and libertarian educational ideas.

At the same time the discourse on migration remains largely a political one in Germany. It is conducted by social scientists and theorists of a so-called multicultural society. Yet knowledge of the culture of the Other remains marginal. While a German author like Martin Walser, even thirty years after the beginning of immigration to Germany, talks of those "billeted with us," it is principally politicians and technocrats who are setting out to find a home for those so billeted.[12] Will this home be called Germany? And if so, on what terms? It is significant that in the German media it is not the arts and culture editors who have taken on the subject of migration but, in the first instance, the political affairs editors. Likewise, German literary criticism lags far behind literary criticism in the United States when it comes to the analysis of the effects of migration on literature. Everything that has to do with the sleeping, dreaming side of humankind, the fertile soil of culture, is underrepresented in German discourse. But where do the images come from that make interaction with the Other possible? Surely not from the Federal German Basic Law [i.e., constitution] or from parliamentary statements. The images of the Other come from memory, from the unconscious, from the sleeping part in us. If we ignore, lose, repress this sleeping part, we run the risk of reducing communication to something to be "dealt with," a task to be carried out—and put behind us.

This practice of "dealing with something" is a source of misunderstandings, fears, and aggressions. The vocabulary word for it in German (*Umgang*) associatively conjures the verbs *um-gehen* and *um-gehen*, that is to say, both "encounter" and "avoid." Until now, the conversations between Turks and Germans have been clumsy attempts on both sides to avoid the Other in the act of encountering him. The result of such encounters is not acquaintance and understanding but fear and aggression. The encounter between Turks and Germans does not only rely on the images that have been passed down; so far, it has also excluded an open debate about these images. Yet politics, which operates with laws and speeches, cannot reduce projections and prejudices, existing fears and aggressions, without reflection on the cultural dimension of Otherness. The question must be asked, Why is it above all Turks who are the targets of arson attacks in Germany? Is it only because the Turks are not yet German citizens? Can the problem really be solved so easily? What does multi-culturalism have to do with culture, if the culture of the Other is completely unknown or familiar only in terms of folklore? The cultural dimension in the migration debate does not mean putting one's hand on the shoulder of the Other or linking arms with him, but listening to him, paying close attention to what goes on inside him, entering a world that, like one's own, is also determined by heritage and memory.

We are indebted to Rudolf Augstein, the editor of the news magazine *Der Spiegel*, for introducing the name of Prince Eugene of Savoy into the debate on dual nationality for Turks in Germany after the murders in Solingen.[13] Invoking Prince Eugene as evidence of the general incompatibility of Turks and Europeans, such as the Germans, reveals a great deal about the sleeping side of Europe. The reactions to Augstein's remarks, on the other hand, were typical of the state of the debate on migration. Instead of considering the possible background to these remarks and bringing one's own sleeping part to consciousness, the enlightened public discussion dismissed Augstein's arguments as the speculations of an old man under the influence of alcohol. Wasn't it curious that only a few months later in Austria letter bombs were sent to individuals in public life, signed with the name "Count von Starhemberg"? (In 1683 Count von Starhemberg was the staunch defender of Vienna against the Turks.) An archaeological excavation of German-Turkish or, better yet, Turkish-European relations did not take place after that either. Yet, in this media age, such historical reminiscences reach adolescents more easily than ever, because they are conveyed not by long-winded history books but by exciting video games in which one can play concentration camp commandant or crusader against the Islamic threat.

At this point it is almost superfluous to say that there is another—Turkish—side to the coin. Since awareness of Turkey, particularly intellectual Turkey, is at a pitifully low and superficial level in Europe, and therefore also in Germany (where not a single translation of work by a contemporary Turkish thinker has been published), not much is known about how the Turkish image of Europe has changed in recent years. From the Turkish perspective, the Europe of the Enlightenment is giving way to an increasingly self-enclosed Christian Europe. Islam and the Ottoman tradition are once again becoming points of reference in the contemporary [Turkish] debate with modernity. If there is no knowledge of Turkish literature, of Turkish thinkers past and present, then public meetings on German-Turkish themes will remain well-meant but largely meaningless encounters. A glance at French bookshops makes plain the poverty of those in Germany. Whereas numerous editions of the work of leading Arab philosophers and writers are available in France, here the interest in Turkey on the part of most German publishers and bookstores is limited to guidebooks.[14]

Samuel Huntington rightly refers to the inherited historical burden in the encounter between Islamic and Western civilization. "Conflict along the fault line between Western and Islamic civilizations has been going on for 1,300 years" (31). "This centuries-old military interaction between the West and Islam is unlikely to decline. It could become more virulent" (31–32).

If we do not know the thought, the literary language, that is, the images and fantasies of the Other, we have no chance of communicating with him in a way that goes beyond "dealing with" the problem. If we keep our own sleeping side under lock and key, we lose the possibility of testing our own prejudices and fears. Is identity anything more than the cage that holds our sleeping side prisoner? There, in our sleeping side, lurks neither a monster of evil nor the Satan of our misdeeds, nor our wheel of fortune. Rather, in it are stored up the crumbs of bread that have been left lying on the scholars' table, the crumbs that have fallen from the artists' files, the words the prophets forgot to communicate to their disciples. They are the formulas of belonging, which the individual always loses and finds again on his way. It is up to us whether we retreat into this side of ourselves or deny it entirely. If we want to communicate with one another, however, in a language that connects as well as separates, then we must confront our consciousness with what comes out of our unconscious.

As long as political, sociological, psychological, and biological components are discussed in the debate on migration, but the culture of the Other, in all its diversity, remains unknown, the migrant can appear only as uprooted. Even the conditions of his uprooting could be understood only if the roots are known. The situation in the countries that are the goal of emigration makes clear, however, that it is not uprooting that is taking place but a transformation of cultural identities. This transformation cannot be grasped without knowledge of the cultural backgrounds of those affected. It is obvious that in countries like Germany, where the cultural background of the immigrants is largely unknown, crude ideas, traditional fears, and projections are spreading that cannot be outweighed by a purely political debate, by expressions of concern and solidarity. It is then only a question of time before the latent violence takes on warlike forms.

The Turks in Germany, of my and future generations, can contribute something to ensuring that what the American foreign policy expert Samuel P. Huntington and the German writer Botho Strauss are predicting—a war in and about civilization—will not take place. For they come from a country that Huntington has described as a torn country. ("The most obvious and prototypical torn country is Turkey" [42].) Some may consider disunity to be a mark of instability. But for someone at home in the metropoles of Europe, which are all torn cities, being torn is a condition that, for the sake of all our futures, has to be accommodated and lived.[15]

Germany long ago became part of us German Turks. Now a question is being posed that we cannot answer alone. Are we also a part of Germany?

1994/1998

Notes

COORDINATES OF ORIENTATION

1. To many participants and observers, the real drama of German unification was signaled by the unexpected opening of the Berlin Wall on November 9, 1989. The Unity Treaty between capitalist Germany and its communist counterpart was signed on August 31, 1990. The agreement terminating the residual rights of the Allied Powers over Germany was signed on September 12, 1990. These accords formally paved the way for the official unification of the German nation on October 3, 1990. (Sometimes the united Federal Republic is referred to as the Berlin Republic, in order to avoid confusion with the Federal Republic that was West Germany until 1990. The national capital of West Germany was Bonn; the national capital of the united Republic is Berlin. This physical relocation of the seat of government has taken nearly a decade to complete.)

2. For insightful descriptions (written in English for a U.S. readership) of many of the problems that prevailed in the early years of unification, see Jane Kramer's essay collection, *The Politics of Memory: Looking for Germany in the New Germany* (New York: Random House, 1996).

3. See Kramer's "Stasi" chapter (*Politics of Memory*, 153–212) for details on the tense atmosphere of moralizing recriminations that attended post-unification revelations about individual East German citizens and their at times convoluted involvement with the state security system of the communist government. (*Stasi*, an abbreviation for *Staatssicherheit[sdienst]*, is the colloquial expression for this surveillance system.) For an excellent discussion of the ways in which West German public debates and values prior to unification were often linked to cultural politics in the GDR, see David Bathrick, *The Powers of Speech: The Politics of Culture in the GDR* (Lincoln: University of Nebraska Press, 1995). Peter Uwe Hohendahl offers a structural account of the German public sphere after unification in his article, "Recasting the Public Sphere," *October* 73 (1995): 27–54. For several incisive essays on related matters, see Andreas Huyssen, *Twilight Memories: Marking Time in a Culture of Amnesia* (New York: Routledge, 1995).

4. See Peter Schneider, *The Wall Jumper*, trans. Leigh Hafrey (New York: Pantheon Books, 1983): "the Wall in our heads" (119). I have used instead the literal translation of the German original.

5. This split vision was, is, and will likely remain one of degree and not of exclusivity.

6. Technically, individuals do not win or lose elections in Germany, but parties do. Helmut Kohl belongs to the centrist Christian Democratic Union (CDU), which is closely allied with the somewhat more conservative Christian Socialist Union (CSU) of Bavaria. Germany's federal chancellor, Gerhard Schröder, belongs to the Social Democratic Party (SPD), which joined with the environmentally conscious Greens (Alliance 90/The Greens) to form the ruling coalition, often referred to as the "red-green" coalition.

7. For more detailed philosophical reflections on imagining relationships between past, present, and future, see Agnes Heller, *A Theory of History* (London: Routledge and Kegan Paul, 1982).

8. The preamble to West Germany's Basic Law (*Grundgesetz*), which functioned for four decades as a kind of temporary constitution, foresaw—as one of its explicit goals—the restoration and preservation of a peaceful, free, and united Germany.

9. Some form of European integration has been a staple of West German policy since its inception. The European Economic Community, of which West Germany was a charter member, was first established by the Treaty of Rome in 1957. This was known as the EEC or the Common Market. In 1967 the EEC was joined with the European Coal and Steel Community and Euratom to form the European Community (EC). The Maastricht Treaty of 1991 gave rise to the European Union (EU). Economic and financial measures have been foregrounded in these agreements. On January 1, 1999, the Euro was introduced as the new currency for eleven participating member nations of the fifteen-member EU (Germany is one of them). After an initial phase of being used for accounting transactions only, the Euro will replace the national currencies of all participating members in 2002.

10. Debates about the proper way to address or interpret the legacy of the Third Reich have taken various forms throughout the history of the Federal Republic, both before and after unification. The German word *Vergangenheitsbewältigung* (overcoming, mastering, or coming to terms with the past) refers to this broad field of thought, affect, and action. For

information in English on some of the key flash points in the 1980s and
1990s, see Geoffrey Hartman, ed., *Bitburg: In Moral and Political Perspec-
tive* (Bloomington: Indiana University Press, 1986); Charles S. Maier, *The
Unmasterable Past: History, Holocaust, and German National Identity*
(Cambridge MA: Harvard University Press, 1988); Robert R. Shandley,
ed., *Unwilling Germans? The Goldhagen Debate*, trans. Jeremiah Riemer
(Minneapolis: University of Minnesota Press, 1998); and Dominick
LaCapra, *History and Memory after Auschwitz* (Ithaca NY: Cornell University Press, 1998). Plans for the National Monument to the Murdered
Jews of Europe (commonly referred to as "the Holocaust Memorial")
originated in the late 1980s on the private initiative of a German talk
show host. They were later endorsed by the federal government under
Kohl and by the Berlin Senate, and a central plot of land near Berlin's
Brandenburg Gate was allocated for this purpose. Several architectural
competitions for the monument's actual design yielded numerous sub-
missions and much disagreement about whether and how to proceed. In
January 1999 the Schröder government approved a modified version of
the site plan that Kohl had hoped to see realized. For more detailed
information and analysis, see James E. Young, *The Texture of Memory:
Holocaust Memorials and Meaning* (New Haven CT: Yale University Press,
1993); James E. Young, ed., *The Art of Memory: Holocaust Memorials in
History* (New York: Prestel, 1994); James E. Young, "Germany's Problems
with Its Holocaust Memorial: A Way Out of the Quagmire?" *Chronicle of
Higher Education* 44.10 (October 13, 1997): B4–B5; Andreas Huyssen,
"Monuments and Holocaust Memory in a Media Age," in *Twilight Memories*, 249–60; and Karen Remmler, "Memorial Spaces and Jewish Identities in Post-Wall Berlin," in *German Cultures/Foreign Cultures: The Politics of Belonging*, ed. Jeffrey Peck, Harry and Helen Gray Humanities
Program Series, vol. 3 (Washington DC: American Institute for Contemporary German Studies, 1998), 41–53.

The novelist Martin Walser was awarded the Peace Prize of the German Book Trade for his many literary successes over time. The presentation of the award in October 1998 and Walser's acceptance speech, which
contained the controversial remarks, were a public event that received
wide media coverage. The most prominent figure to challenge Walser's
polemics on Auschwitz was Ignatz Bubis, a Holocaust survivor and, from
1992 until his death in 1999, the head of the Central Council of Jews in
Germany. The full German text of Walser's acceptance speech, along with

Frank Schirrmacher's *laudatio*, is available in a 1998 publication by Suhr-kamp under the title *Erfahrungen beim Verfassen einer Sonntagsrede*. The passage in which Walser argues that references to Auschwitz should not be used as a routinized means of moral intimidation can be found on page 20 of that text.

11. It should be superfluous to note that the German nation and its people are no less complex than any others. Given the historical burden of the Third Reich, World War II, and the Holocaust, however, critical voices since 1945, both inside and outside Germany, have been particularly sensitive to any societal developments that hint at any neofascist poten-tial. The 1930s and 1940s might thus be seen in the postwar era as what Agnes Heller calls a "past-present age," that is to say, "an age whose symbols and values have become *meaningful* for us. It can threaten us or fill us with hopes even if it is beyond our power to alter it" (*A Theory of History*, 44). Although leftist student activists of the late 1960s liked to decry capitalist Germany as a "fascist" state, Heller's notion of a "past-present age" does not at all suggest a concrete, structural analogy be-tween one historical phenomenon and another. Instead, it connotes the largely *symbolic* capacity of an age that no longer exists to seize those living in the present with either hope or dread. These affective options need not be mutually exclusive, as the age of the American Revolution might demonstrate. We no longer live in that historical past, but life in the United States today continues to be infused with the inspirational legacy of individual rights and also haunted by the racist legacy of slavery and genocide. For additional comments on Heller's theory of history, especially with reference to modern Germany, see Leslie A. Adelson, *Making Bodies, Making History: Feminism and German Identity* (Lincoln: University of Nebraska Press, 1993), 23–27. One might also think of the GDR as a "past-present age" in this symbolic sense.

12. Joyce Marie Mushaben, *From Post-War to Post-Wall Generations: Chang-ing Attitudes toward the National Question and* NATO *in the Federal Re-public of Germany* (Boulder CO: Westview Press, 1998), 329.

13. Where does violence begin or end? This is an important philosophical question that I cannot begin to address here. For present purposes the term is used in its mundane, pragmatic sense, to characterize incidents in which persons perceived to be racially or ethnically different (from per-sons deemed to be German) were physically attacked.

14. Mushaben, *From Post-War to Post-Wall Generations*, 329. For an anthro-

pologist's reflections on post-unification violence by right-wing groups, left-wing groups, and unaffiliated individuals, see Uli Linke, "Violence, Memory, and Selfhood in Germany," *New German Critique* 64 (1995): 37–60.

15. See Mushaben, *From Post-War to Post-Wall Generations*, 346, for a summary of the criminal findings in English. For an extensive German-language account of the Solingen case, see Metin Gür and Alaverdi Turhan, *Die Solingen-Akte*, trans. Hartwig Mau (Düsseldorf: Patmos, 1996). Hajo Funke has called the *Lichterketten* (chains of light) "the largest citizens' initiative in Germany since 1945." See his study of right-wing extremism, *Brandstifter: Deutschland zwischen Demokratie und völkischem Nationalismus* (Göttingen: Lamuv, 1993), 9. From an anthropological perspective, Uli Linke examines the cultural significance of fire in the last chapter of her *German Bodies: Race and Representation after Hitler* (New York: Routledge, 1999).

16. The German original can be found in an interview conducted by Feridun Zaimoğlu with "Zeynep," published in the interviewer's most recent book, *Koppstoff: Kanaka Sprak vom Rande der Gesellschaft* (Berlin: Rotbuch, 1998), 82.

17. The German word for foreigners is *Ausländer*, literally "out-landers."

18. See Mushaben's chapter on "What It Means to Be *Non-German*" (*From Post-War to Post-Wall Generations*, 315–59) for additional details and background information on incidents in Hoyerswerda, Rostock, Mölln, Solingen, and elsewhere.

19. One of the organizations that continues to track incidents of xenophobic and racist violence since unification is the RAA in Berlin, under the direction of Anetta Kahane (RAA stands for *Regionale Arbeitsstellen für Ausländerfragen, Jugendarbeit und Schule*, or Regional Offices for Work on Issues Pertaining to Foreigners, Youth, and Education). The RAA also takes a proactive stance, developing educational fora and materials to promote alternatives to violence. In 1997, for example, the RAA designed and made available two computerized action games, Bren and Courage, as alternatives to youth entertainment that celebrates violence and encourages racism. RAA materials may be obtained from the Berlin office, Schumannstrasse 5, D-10117 Berlin.

20. For more detailed statistics see especially Wesley D. Chapin, "The Turkish Diaspora in Germany," *Diaspora* 5 (1996): 275–301; David Horrocks and Eva Kolinsky, eds., *Turkish Culture in German Society Today* (Provi-

dence RI: Berghahn, 1996); and Mushaben, *From Post-War to Post-Wall Generations.*

21. These are some of the most common terms and points of reference that one finds in public debates and discourses about Germany, modernity, and democracy. One might of course ask whether Germany's citizenship law is necessarily, in and of itself, an appropriate or a sufficient test of the country's commitment to democratic principles.

22. For some of the broader political, philosophical, and ethical issues informing debates on migration and citizenship in Germany and Europe, see William A. Barbieri Jr., *Ethics of Citizenship: Immigration and Group Rights in Germany* (Durham NC: Duke University Press, 1998), and Yasemin Nuhoğlu Soysal, *Limits of Citizenship: Migrants and Postnational Membership in Europe* (Chicago: University of Chicago Press, 1994). Both studies provide extensive bibliographies that will direct interested readers to additional sources. Mushaben (*From Post-War to Post-Wall Generations*, 316–25) offers a succinct review of German citizenship law and asylum policy, including lesser and greater changes in both over the last decade. For English-language accounts of how these laws have affected Turkish individuals and communities in Germany, see the various articles in Horrocks and Kolinsky, *Turkish Culture in German Society Today*, and also Chapin, "The Turkish Diaspora." Additionally one may consult Wesley D. Chapin, *Germany for the Germans? The Political Effects of International Migration* (Westport CT: Greenwood Press, 1997).

23. This unsigned commentary appears in "Turkish Germans?" *The Economist* (Janunary 9, 1999), 17. In spite of the postunification violence against foreigners described above, the Federal Republic did indeed espouse the most liberal asylum policy in Europe. As Article 16 of the Basic Law stipulated, "Those who are politically persecuted have the right to asylum." This article stood from 1949 until 1993, when some formal restrictions were established in an atmosphere of highly charged public debate.

24. Barbieri, *Ethics of Citizenship*, 26.

25. The German word for such migrants is *Aussiedler* (those who settled "out"). *Umsiedler* (those who settled "over") refers to East German citizens who somehow managed to move to the West while the country was still divided. West German citizenship was automatically extended to East Germans who wanted and found a way to claim it.

26. On the latter phenomenon see Stanford J. Shaw, *Turkey and the Holo-*

caust: Turkey's Role in Rescuing Turkish and European Jewry from Nazi Persecution, 1933–1945 (New York: New York University Press, 1993). Sargut Şölçün sketches centuries of Turkish-European relations in *Sein und Nichtsein: Zur Literatur in der multikulturellen Gesellschaft* (Bielefeld: Aisthesis, 1992). For an English-language review of this study, see my remarks in *German Quarterly* 67 (1994): 283–84.

27. See Klaus Grosch, "Foreigners and Aliens," in *Meet United Germany: Perspectives*, ed. Susan Stern (Frankfurt a.M.: Frankfurter Allgemeine Zeitung, 1991), 231–45, here 233. For additional details and more extensive analysis of this and related phenomena, see Chapin, *Germany for the Germans?*

28. William M. Chandler, "Immigration Politics and Citizenship in Germany," in *The Federal Republic of Germany at Forty-Five: Union without Unity*, ed. Peter H. Merkl (New York: New York University Press, 1995), 344–56, here 347.

29. See Erik J. Zürcher, *Turkey: A Modern History* (London: Tauris, 1993), 282–85. For other historical overviews of modern Turkey, see Feroz Ahmad, *The Making of Modern Turkey* (London: Routledge, 1993), and Nicole and Hugh Pope, *Turkey Unveiled: Atatürk and After* (London: Murray, 1997).

30. Horrocks and Kolinsky, "Introduction: Migrants or Citizens? Turks in Germany between Exclusion and Acceptance," in *Turkish Culture in German Society Today*, x–xxviii, here xviii.

31. One Green representative of the German parliament has published his Turkish-German autobiography with the title *Ich bin Inländer: Ein anatolischer Schwabe im Bundestag* [I am an In-Lander: An Anatolian Swabian in Parliament], as told to Hans Engels (Munich: dtv, 1997). (*Inländer* is a pointed alternative to *Ausländer*, the standard German word for "foreigner." The references to Anatolia and Swabia stress regional affinities rather than national markers of identity.) Son of a *Gastarbeiter*, Cem Özdemir was born in West Germany in 1965. After applying for German citizenship at the age of sixteen, the would-be environmental activist became a German citizen in 1983. This process and the political career that followed are described in his German-language autobiography, as are various reactions among Özdemir's friends, relatives, colleagues, and constituents. Another example would be the Turkish-born professor of political science, Hakkı Keskin, who has been especially active in Hamburg politics.

32. See Gerald L. Neuman, "Nationality Law in the United States and the Federal Republic of Germany: Structure and Current Problems," in *Paths to Inclusion: The Integration of Migrants in the United States and Germany*, ed. Peter H. Schuck and Rainer Münz (New York: Berghahn, 1998), 247–97, here 265. *Paths to Inclusion* is volume 5 in a Berghahn series, edited by Myron Weiner, that takes a comparative legal, political, and sociological approach to migrants and refugees in the United States and Germany (the full title of the series is *Migration and Refugees: Politics and Policies in the United States and Germany*). All five volumes are especially recommended to readers who would like to know more about similarities and differences between German and U.S. public policies regarding foreigners. Volume 1 in the series is *Migration Past, Migration Future: Germany and the United States*, ed. Klaus J. Bade and Myron Weiner (1997); volume 2 is *Migrants, Refugees, and Foreign Policy: U.S. and German Policies toward Countries of Origin*, ed. Rainer Münz and Myron Weiner (1997); volume 3 is *Immigration Admissions: The Search for Workable Policies in Germany and the United States*, ed. Kay Hailbronner, David A. Martin, and Hiroshi Motomura (1997); and volume 4 is *Immigration Controls: The Search for Workable Policies in Germany and the United States*, ed. Kay Hailbronner, David A. Martin, and Hiroshi Motomura (1998). The Neuman essay in *Paths to Inclusion* ("Nationality Law in the United States and the Federal Republic of Germany") provides an especially helpful account of significant features of and decisive changes in German citizenship law prior to 1998. For those readers interested in a more general picture of issues that have concerned the Federal Republic in the 1990s, see two anthologies edited by Peter H. Merkl, *The Federal Republic of Germany at Forty* (New York: New York University Press, 1989) and *The Federal Republic of Germany at Forty-Five: Union without Unity* (New York: New York University Press, 1995). (The latter contains William M. Chandler's article on "Immigration Politics and Citizenship," mentioned earlier.) On the subject of European and international contexts in which Turkish migration may also be understood, interested readers may consult Stephen Castles, Heather Booth, and Tina Wallace, eds., *Here for Good: Western Europe's New Ethnic Minorities* (New York: Greenwood Press, 1984), and Stephen Castles and Mark J. Miller, eds., *The Age of Migration: International Population Movements in the Modern World* (New York: Guilford, 1993).

33. Neuman, "Nationality Law in the United States and the Federal Republic

of Germany," 250. See also William Rogers Brubaker, *Citizenship and Nationhood in France and Germany* (Cambridge MA: Harvard University Press, 1992).

34. These were of course not the only requirements to be met. Some of the other major requirements concerned financial self-sufficiency, untarnished moral character, fluency in German, and formal release from prior national obligations and loyalties. Applicants usually also had to demonstrate that they had lived in the Federal Republic for ten years or more (for certain groups the residency requirement was fifteen years). See Neuman, "Nationality Law," for details.

35. When used in reference to Turkish residents in Germany, the term "national minority" relies on the more pragmatic sense of the word "national," not the culturally laden sense that has accrued to *Nation* in German history. That is to say, this "national minority" is a minority of individuals who hold passports from the Republic of Turkey. Although many Germans think of all Turks as sharing the same ethnicity, the word "ethnic" would not be a suitable substitute for "national" here, because several different ethnic groups (e.g., Turks, Kurds, Armenians) have Turkish passports and are considered "Turks" in Germany. Some of these ethnic distinctions have extremely serious political implications in Turkey, Germany, and elsewhere. See Ralf Goldak, "Thinking the Kurdish Diaspora in Germany: A Critical Inquiry," Ph.D. diss., University of Wales, Aberystwyth, 1997, on the German situation in particular.

36. Neuman, "Nationality Law," 263.

37. Neuman ("Nationality Law," 266–68) enumerates these revisions in some detail. Some of the modifications allowed for relaxed requirements for members of the older generation who had lived in the Federal Republic, without a criminal record, for fifteen years. Others sought to make naturalization easier for members of the younger generations who had lived in Germany for eight years and were between the ages of sixteen and twenty-three at the time of application. In 1993 one important reform made naturalization in most instances an entitlement rather than a discretionary matter in the hands of the bureaucrat handling the application. (In other words, an applicant who met the criteria for naturalization had a legal right to citizenship and could appeal to that right if an individual bureaucrat ruled unfavorably on the application.)

38. See Neuman, "Nationality Law," 275, 280.

39. Neuman and other scholars to whom he refers make this observation as well ("Nationality Law," 275).

40. This information is culled from various news sources but especially from the January 15, 1999, issue of *Deutschland Nachrichten*, distributed electronically by the German Information Center in New York City to its e-mail subscriber list.

41. Foreigners will be eligible to apply for citizenship after eight years of lawful residency. Previously, a minimum residency of fifteen years was required for some.

42. The specific nature and extent of political rights for Turks in Germany are clearly subject to debate, while reasonable guarantees of physical safety should be a given.

43. The main title for this collection of essays, which have been selected from several different publications, derives from the German title of the author's first volume of published essays, *Atlas des tropischen Deutschland: Essays* (Berlin: Babel, 1992). For the English-language publication I have used *Atlas of a Tropical Germany* rather than *Atlas of the Tropical Germany*. The indefinite article sounds better in the English translation, and its implications are more in tune with the author's actual arguments, which do not assign "tropicality" to a fixed population group or geographical location.

44. I have translated these slogans from a newspaper article on the petition campaign. See Tom Schimmeck, "Umschalten von Kopf auf Bauch," *Die Woche*, January 22, 1999, 8–9, here 9.

45. I have adapted Bernard Lewis's phrase ("the heart of Christian Europe") for my own purposes here. In his book, *Islam and the West* (New York: Oxford University Press, 1993), he writes of premodern conflicts: "For a century and a half, the Turkish armies, operating from their bases in Buda and Belgrade, offered a nearer and greater threat to the heart of Christian Europe than had ever come from the Saracens in Spain" (11). Lewis uses "heart" metaphorically to refer to geographical regions that were centrally located in what came to be known as Christian Europe. My use of the word shifts the metaphor to the affective symbolic realm, a discursive linkage that Şenocak's essays prod and probe critically in more detail. Readers interested in European discourses of "the Orient" more generally should of course consult Edward W. Said's ground-breaking study, *Orientalism* (New York: Pantheon, 1978). Scholarly responses to both Said and Lewis, and to the sharply worded disagreements between them, are far too numerous to be listed here.

46. Adelson, "Opposing Oppositions: Turkish-German Questions in Contemporary German Studies," *German Studies Review* 17 (1994): 303–30, here 308–9. Many other factors are of course also involved. The one most frequently cited by Europeans is Turkey's human rights record. Turkish politicians have, on the other hand, been greatly offended by Europe's ongoing rejection of the Republic of Turkey as a candidate for EU membership. At times this resentment has coincided with Turkish responses in Germany to antiforeigner sentiment there.

47. The 1991 Gulf War ignited a crisis of conscience among many German intellectuals, especially on the Left and for longtime pacifists. As Kizer Walker explains: "In the months preceding the bombardment of Iraq by the United States and its allies, details surfaced about the extent of German contributions to Baghdad's chemical arms program. Not only was German industry reckoned to have been responsible, through technical assistance and the delivery of materials, for some 90 percent of Iraq's capability to produce chemical weapons; German firms were also involved in reoutfitting Soviet SCUDs to bring Israel into range of these weapons. The firms involved in this project were guaranteed protection against financial loss by the Kohl administration. The prospect that survivors of Auschwitz could in 1991 be gassed by a collusion of German capital and the German state pushed Israel to the center of the Gulf conflict in the German discourse and tore up lines of political allegiances in Germany." See Walker, "The Persian Gulf War and the Germans' 'Jewish Questions': Transformations on the Left," in *Reemerging Jewish Culture in Germany: Life and Literature since 1989*, ed. Sander L. Gilman and Karen Remmler (New York: New York University Press, 1994), 148–69, here 149–50. Additional controversy circled around the question of possible deployment of German troops, a move long subject to rigorous constitutional restraints. After some initial hesitation, Kohl authorized financial subsidies and logistical support for Allied efforts against Iraq: "some 3,200 German soldiers were soon stationed in Turkey and the Mediterranean, the largest such mobilization since 1945" (Walker, "The Persian Gulf War," 151). For additional commentary in English on the Persian Gulf War of 1991 and German politics, see Anson Rabinbach, "German Intellectuals and the Gulf War," *Dissent* 38 (fall 1991): 459–63, and Russell A. Berman, "The Gulf War and Intellectuals, in Germany and the United States," *Telos* 88 (summer 1991): 167–79.

48. The Republic of Turkey, founded by Mustafa Kemal Atatürk in 1923, is

decidedly secular in its orientation. The modern Turkish military, which has recently taken action to limit the political activities of Islamic parties with a blatantly religious agenda, has traditionally been the staunch defender of Turkish Republican values. Many Turks in Turkey are committed secularists. Many are practicing Muslims. Being a Muslim in Turkey does not necessarily mean that one desires the overthrow of secularism. Debates between secularists and religious fundamentalists have nonetheless grown more tense in the 1990s. See Zürcher, *Turkey: A Modern History*, for historical background to relevant controversies. For an excellent article on the quite varied function of Islam for Germany's resident Turks, see Yasemin Karakasoğlu, "Turkish Cultural Orientations in Germany and the Role of Islam," in Horrocks and Kolinsky, eds., *Turkish Culture in German Society Today*, 157–79.

49. In an article taken to task in the final essay of this *Atlas*, Samuel P. Huntington argues, "The Velvet Curtain of culture has replaced the Iron Curtain of ideology as the most significant dividing line of Europe." See "The Clash of Civilizations?" *Foreign Affairs* 72.3 (1993): 22–49, here 31. For reasons that become clear in the essays themselves, Şenocak's understanding of the current situation differs radically from that presented by Huntington. The latter's concept of a "Velvet Curtain" does not apply.

50. Dreaming is also an important motif in Şenocak's essays and literary prose.

51. Again, the extent of Said's influence on scholarly discussions of Orientalist discourse cannot be overestimated. For seminal studies on rhetoric, narrative, and history as a "poetic" discourse, see Hayden White's *Metahistory* (Baltimore: Johns Hopkins University Press, 1973), *Tropics of Discourse* (Baltimore: Johns Hopkins University Press, 1978), *The Content of the Form* (Baltimore: Johns Hopkins University Press, 1987), and *Figural Realism: Studies in the Mimesis Effect* (Baltimore: Johns Hopkins University Press, 1999). Although Zafer Şenocak's critical interventions as a public intellectual are unique in Germany, similar "tropical" questions and allusions can be found in many other contexts where migrant cultures and postcolonial discourses are at stake. Salman Rushdie, possibly the most famous contemporary writer to make these issues into the stuff of his novels, imagines London as "a tropical city" in *The Satanic Verses* (London: Viking, 1988), 354. (Şenocak also cites this passage from the novel in the original version of his essay "The Poet and the Deserters.") *The Satanic Verses* is the explosive work of fiction that incurred the wrath

of the Ayatollah Khomeini. On the basis of what the revolutionary political and religious leader of Iran deemed a blasphemous treatment of Islam, he condemned Rushdie to death on February 14, 1989, calling on all Muslims to kill the Bombay-born author living in self-imposed British exile. Although Rushdie is still alive, the late Ayatollah's religious sentence or *fatwa* was not officially rescinded by the Iranian government until 1998. While it was still in force, Rushdie lived in hiding with the help of the British government. The entanglement of politics and culture was in this instance formidable. For analysis of Rushdie's literary projects, interested readers may wish to consult Timothy Brennan, *Salman Rushdie and the Third World: Myths of the Nation* (New York: St. Martin's, 1989), and Aijaz Ahmad, *In Theory: Classes, Nations, Literatures* (London: Verso, 1992). Ahmad also includes a critical chapter on Said (*"Orientalism* and After," 159–219).

52. Mushaben, *From Post-War to Post-Wall Generations*, 5.

53. Recent interviews conducted by Feridun Zaimoğlu are perhaps symptomatic of one facet of differences between the third generation and those that came before. See his *Kanak Sprak: 24 Mißtöne vom Rande der Gesellschaft* [Kanak talk: 24 harsh notes from society's edge] (Berlin: Rotbuch, 1995), which includes interviews with men only, and *Koppstoff* [Head Stuff], which focuses on young women. These books have made Zaimoğlu, who moved to Germany in 1968 at the age of four, something of a cult star. At the same time, it should be noted that none of his books speaks or could speak for an entire generation. Differences between generations are compounded by differences within each generation. On November 27–29, 1998, a conference devoted to Turkish-German culture of the second and third generations took place at the University of Wales at Swansea. The conference organizer, Tom Cheesman, is preparing the proceedings for publication. The conference program, "Postmigrant Turkish-German Culture: Transnationalism, Translation, Politics of Representation," was posted on the World Wide Web at ⟨http://www.swan.ac.uk/german/axial/postmig/prog.htm⟩. Comparative in its conceptualization, the "Axial Writing" research project on transnational literary cultures deals with Turkish, South Asian, Caribbean, and Irish diaspora cultures. Based at the University of Oxford, the project is part of the Transnational Communities Research Programme (1998–2003) funded by the United Kingdom Economic and Social Research Council. For more information visit ⟨http://www.transcomm.ox.ac.uk⟩.

54. These terms are of limited use in steering readers who are unfamiliar with Germany past the customary touchstones of "cultural difference" between Germans and Turks. Şenocak himself is only one example of a German who is also a Turk. For a superb study of crosscultural identifications over successive generations on three different continents between the eighteenth century and 1945, see Leo Spitzer, *Lives in Between: Assimilation and Marginality in Austria, Brazil, West Africa, 1780–1945* (Cambridge: Cambridge University Press, 1989). Although Spitzer does not deal with Turkish lives or the contemporary era that concerns us here, his book will appeal to anyone grappling with comparable structural and methodological challenges. Its lucid complexity and substantive range of insights are unsurpassed.

55. One anecdote may serve to illustrate a "diplomatic" German form of this. Speaking at Cornell University shortly before the federal elections in September 1998, His Excellency Jürgen Chrobog, the Federal Republic's ambassador to the United States, lectured on European integration (by which he meant relations among EU member nations). During the question-and-answer period I asked if he would comment on the issue of integration *within* Germany, especially regarding Turkish residents there. The ambassador's immediate response was simply to repeat what he had already said about the Republic of Turkey in his formal presentation, namely, that it was a close friend and partner and important in NATO, but not yet ready to be admitted to the EU.

   The ambassador also emphasized that the EU is not a Christian organization or a religious organization at all. Because of this, he cautioned, the EU's rejection of Turkey cannot be attributed to any purported religious criteria for inclusion. This diplomatic distinction differs considerably from political and journalistic language common in earlier years, when the adjectives "democratic," "European," and "Christian" were often linked with reference to the EC and the EU. When Şenocak refers to the EU in his "crossroads" essay as a "Christian club," he has this discursive tradition in mind.

56. One volatile example of the "enclave" approach to Turkish-German relations was provided in early June 1998, when Berlin media were filled with heated debates triggered by a newspaper interview with the minister for Internal Affairs for the city of Berlin (published in the BZ on June 2). Commenting on policies pertaining to foreigners in Berlin, Jörg Schönbohm had decried the existence of "parallel societies" in Berlin, intoler-

able foreign "ghettos" where "one is not located in Germany" (my translation from the German, as cited in the *tageszeitung* [Berlin], June 3, 1998, 1). One of the most critical responses to Schönbohm (among many across the political spectrum, including Schönbohm's own party) came from the head of Berlin's Jewish community, Andreas Nachama, who accused the CDU politician of an ideological proximity to the Nazis of yesteryear. (Nachama's initial commentary can be found in the *Tagesspiegel* [Berlin], June 10, 1998, 11.) Schönbohm's highly controversial remarks referred especially to sections of Berlin that are predominantly populated by Turks. Kreuzberg is the most famous of these.

Given that Germans often say that Turks like to "keep to themselves" and then regard this as a sign of Turks' inability to "integrate" into Germany society, we should pause to consider a thorny methodological question. Even if many Turks in some German cities do prefer to live in neighborhoods where Turks and other "foreigners" also reside, can we necessarily conclude that "cultural difference" can be located there? Does the physical site that one inhabits really determine all the points of orientation that shape a human life, for an individual or for a community? With these and related questions in mind, one political scientist at the University of Hannover has addressed a problem in much empirical research done on Turkish migrants in the Federal Republic. If one allows for "ghettoization" and "full assimilation" as the only two possible options for socialization, he explains, then one can neither imagine nor recognize the much wider and more complex range of interactions that make up the lives of most resident Turks. For this reason he finds it more accurate to speak of Turkish *communities* in Germany (he uses the English word), not the *ghettos* that inflamed Schönbohm's imagination. See Günter Max Behrendt, "Die türkischen *communities* von Hannover," in *Brücken zwischen Zivilisationen: Zur Zivilisierung ethnisch-kultureller Differenzen und Machtungleichheiten/Das türkische Beispiel*, ed. Hans-Peter Waldhoff, Dursun Tan, and Elçin Kürşat-Ahlers (Frankfurt a.M.: IKO, 1997), 213–34. This interdisciplinary anthology represents an important scholarly attempt to break some of the stereotypical molds that "Turks in Germany" are too often made to fit. The book also contains an unusually good sociobiographical and cultural commentary on Zafer Şenocak, whom Hans-Peter Waldhoff sees as a practitioner of "a transnational mode of thought." See Waldhoff, "Ein Übersetzer: Über die soziobiographische Genese eines transnationalen Denkstils" (323–64). At the

113

end of his essay he alludes to more extensive, as yet unpublished work, in which he will analyze something that he calls *fremddenken* [thinking strange]: "something third, something ambivalent, something capable of ambivalence" (364).

57. "Seljukian Anatolia" refers to a time before the Ottoman Empire, when Turkish dynasties ruled between the eleventh and thirteenth centuries. "Moorish Spain" is the term that Europeans have traditionally used for the eight centuries during which Muslim rulers controlled the Iberian peninsula (from c. 700 on). (The region had been conquered by North Africans of Arab and Berber descent, whom the Spaniards dubbed "Moors.") This period came to an end in 1492, after which notoriously intolerant Christian monarchs reigned. The names of King Ferdinand and Queen Isabella will no doubt be familiar to many American readers as those who financed Christopher Columbus's famous and consequential voyages. In 1492 they also authorized the expulsion of Spain's Muslims and Jews.

58. The definite article in "the Islamic world" belongs to a figure of speech, a figure of convenience but of questionable accuracy. Where could one locate a monolithic entity such as "the Islamic world" or "the Christian world"? What kind of imaginative map would we have to draw to account for one space inhabited by more than one "world"?

The Western designation for Ibn Rushd (1126–98) has conventionally been Averroës, and Ibn Sina (980–1037) is known to the West as Avicenna. Physician and philosopher, the latter commented extensively on the imaginative and "civil purpose" of poetry and rhetoric and on Aristotle in particular. His medical writings retained their authority for centuries. Born in Andalusian Spain, Ibn Rushd was trained in theology, law, philosophy, and medicine. His philosophical oeuvre stressed empiricism and rationality, and his commentaries on Aristotle were regarded as authoritative in medieval times. According to Aijaz Ahmad, "a great many European thinkers" found their way to Greek philosophy mediated "through their encounter with the labours of men like Ibn Rushd and Ibn Sina" (Ahmad, *In Theory*, 188).

59. Adelson, "Opposing Oppositions," includes a discussion of Sten Nadolny's *Selim oder die Gabe der Rede* (Munich: Piper, 1990), which was the first German novel to participate in this creative project, broadly understood.

60. See "Between Orient and Occident." Şenocak's German coinage is "*eine*

Berührungsgeschichte zwischen Orient und Okzident." The inference of a "sixth" historical sense is mine. For additional commentary on history as a kind of sixth sense, see the social theoretical reflections of Oskar Negt and Alexander Kluge, *Geschichte und Eigensinn* (Frankfurt a.M.: Zweitausendeins, 1981), as discussed in Adelson, *Making Bodies*, 11–13. Negt and Kluge do not, however, address the specific histories that concern Şenocak here.

61. This volume closes with "War and Peace in Modernity," which entails a pointed critique of Samuel P. Huntington's theses on the "clash of civilizations," first published in English as "The Clash of Civilizations?" *Foreign Affairs* 72.3 (1993): 22–49. Three years later Huntington's expanded and immensely controversial analysis of "cultural" conflict appeared as *The Clash of Civilizations and the Remaking of World Order* (New York: Simon and Schuster, 1996). The German translation of this book was published as *Kampf der Kulturen/The Clash of Civilizations: Die Neugestaltung der Weltpolitik im 21. Jahrhundert*, trans. H. Fliessbach (Munich: Europa, 1996). Most of "War and Peace in Modernity" was written in response to Huntington's initial article, but Şenocak added several paragraphs in 1998, after the translation of Huntington's work into German had prompted a wider reception of it in the Federal Republic, where "the Turks" currently occupy the exemplary space of the presumed cultural Other.

62. The title of Strauss's essay does not lend itself readily to English translation. *Gesang* is a noun referring to song or a certain kind of recited poetry. *Bock*, also a noun, denotes a male member of a horned or antlered species. The present participle *anschwellend* functions here as an adjective meaning *swelling* or *rising*. One might then translate the essay title as "Ram's Bugling Call, Rising." The image suggests an animal targeted for sacrifice but gradually voicing resistance to being offered up in such a fashion, an unwilling scapegoat, as it were. In a densely worded attack on liberal German self-hatred in the postwar period, this discussion of *German* "scapegoats" was bound to touch a raw nerve. "*Anschwellender Bocksgesang*" originally appeared in *Spiegel* 47.6 (February 8, 1993): 202–7. It was reprinted in the anthology *Die selbstbewußte Nation: "Anschwellender Bocksgesang" und weitere Beiträge zu einer deutschen Debatte*, ed. Heimo Schwilk and Ulrich Schacht (Berlin: Ullstein, 1994), 19–40. For critical assessments of this essay, the debate it sparked, and its relationship to Strauss's literary oeuvre, see the special journal issue on Botho Strauss edited by Sigrid Berka, *Weimarer Beiträge* 40.2 (1994).

63. I rely here on Martin Chalmers's English translation of the Strauss original, as cited in Chalmers's translation of "War and Peace in Modernity" for *Cultural Studies* 10 (1996): 255–69, here 263.

64. Huntington ("The Clash of Civilizations?" 41, 48) also borrows a phrase from the title of Kishore Mahbubani's article "The West and the Rest," *The National Interest* 28 (summer 1992): 3–13. Under the rubric of non-Western civilization Huntington lists, for example, "Islamic, Confucian, Japanese, Hindu, Buddhist or Orthodox cultures" (40). Şenocak's essay "War and Peace in Modernity" focuses on Huntington's comments about Islam and Turkey in particular.

65. In addition to Said's *Orientalism*, readers may wish to consult one of his later books, *Covering Islam: How the Media and the Experts Determine How We See the Rest of the World* (1981; New York: Vintage Books, 1997). For an overview of the theories espoused and influence exerted by Foucault, Said, and the other thinkers mentioned in this paragraph, see the relevant entries in Michael Groden and Martin Kreiswirth, eds., *The Johns Hopkins Guide to Literary Theory and Criticism* (Baltimore: Johns Hopkins University Press, 1994). Under Walid Hamarneh's entry "Arabic Theory and Criticism" the *Guide* also provides useful information on Ibn Sina and Ibn Rushd, mentioned earlier.

66. Generally speaking, hermeneutics refers to the theory of interpretation and understanding. For useful overviews of nineteenth- and twentieth-century hermeneutics, see the relevant entries by Tilottama Rajan and Robert C. Holub in *The Johns Hopkins Guide to Literary Theory and Criticism*.

67. Paul Celan (1920–70) was born as Paul Antschel (Ancel) to German-speaking Jewish parents in the Bucovina region of Romania. Unlike many other European Jews, including his parents, Celan survived the war and Nazi persecution, only to take his own life in Paris decades later. His linguistically complex, often mystical poetry, which he composed in German, is widely honored for its great art and anguish. Celan's single best known poem is *Todesfuge* ("Death Fugue") from 1945, which contains the famous line, "death is a master from Germany." See *The Poems of Paul Celan*, trans. Michael Hamburger (New York: Persea, 1988), 63. Hamburger's introduction (17–32) provides additional commentary on Celan's biography and poetry. Şenocak alludes most specifically to *Die Niemandsrose* [The no one's rose], a volume of poetry first published in 1963.

68. For comparative reflections in English on Turks and Jews in the Federal Republic, see Jeffrey Peck, "Turks and Jews: Comparing Minorities in Germany after the Holocaust," in *German Cultures, Foreign Cultures: The Politics of Belonging*, ed. Jeffrey Peck, Harry and Helen Gray Humanities Program Series, vol. 3 (Washington DC: American Institute for Contemporary German Studies, 1998), 1–16. One chapter of my book in progress on Turkish-German literature will more specifically address "Touching Tales of Turks, Germans, and Jews: Cultural Alterity, Historical Narrative, and Literary Riddles for the '90s," especially as they figure in Şenocak's literary prose. For a discussion of Jews in unified Germany, see Sander L. Gilman, *Jews in Today's German Culture* (Bloomington: Indiana University Press, 1995). Readers may also wish to consult two earlier articles by Gilman ("Jewish Writers in Contemporary Germany" and "German Reunification and the Jews") in a volume that he coedited with Steven T. Katz, *Anti-Semitism in Times of Crisis* (New York: New York University Press, 1991). See Michael Brenner, *After the Holocaust: Rebuilding Jewish Lives in Postwar Germany*, trans. Barbara Harshav (Princeton NJ: Princeton University Press, 1997), for a lively historical account of the period between 1945 and unification.

69. See n. 10.

70. See "The Poet and the Deserters" for Şenocak's explicit remarks on Rushdie in this regard.

71. Mapping metaphors have obviously guided me in writing this introduction, largely because Şenocak's titles, topics, and language seem to demand them. At the same time, I should note that the history and discourse of cartography are themselves riddled with political pitfalls. For example, Russell A. Berman's recent study *Enlightenment or Empire: Colonial Discourse in German Culture* (Lincoln: University of Nebraska Press, 1998) associates Captain Cook's eighteenth-century cartography of the South Seas with instrumental rationality and potential exploitation, in contrast to Georg Forster's emancipatory philosophy of enlightened inclusion ("The Enlightenment Travelogue and the Colonial Text," 21–64). The kind of cartography that Şenocak has in mind, however, is quite different from the sort that Berman ascribes to Cook. Şenocak's atlas is itself a metaphor, not a sheet of paper. His essays rely on and promote multiple coordinates of orientation, not the reductive flatness of dichotomous dimensions.

72. See Adelson, "Opposing Oppositions," 321–22, n. 1, for a long list of

secondary sources in German and English on the development of "guest worker literature" and "migrants' literature" in German. Especially helpful commentaries in English and additional references may be found in Arlene Akiko Teraoka, "*Gastarbeiterliteratur*: The Other Speaks Back," *Cultural Critique* 7 (1987): 77–101; Arlene Akiko Teraoka, "Talking 'Turk': On Narrative Strategies and Cultural Stereotypes," *New German Critique* 46 (1989): 104–28; Ülker Gökberk, "Understanding Alterity: *Ausländerliteratur* between Relativism and Universalism," in *Theoretical Issues in Literary History*, ed. David Perkins, Harvard English Studies, vol. 16 (Cambridge MA: Harvard University Press, 1991), 143–72; Heidrun Suhr, "*Ausländerliteratur*: Minority Literature in the Federal Republic of Germany," *New German Critique* 46 (1989): 71–103; and Azade Seyhan, "Scheherazade's Daughters: The Thousand and One Tales of Turkish-German Women Writers," in *Writing New Identities: Gender, Nation, and Immigration in Contemporary Europe*, ed. Gisela Brinker-Gabler and Sidonie Smith (Minneapolis: University of Minnesota Press, 1997), 230–48. (Teraoka's "Talking 'Turk'" is reprinted in her book *East, West, and Others: The Third World in Postwar German Literature* [Lincoln: University of Nebraska Press, 1996], 135–61.) For an excellent overview of this cultural development in the broader context of West German literature after 1945, see Moray McGowan, "German Writing in the West (1945–1990)," in *The Cambridge History of German Literature*, ed. Helen Watanabe-O'Kelly (Cambridge: Cambridge University Press, 1997), 440–506.

73. Claus Leggewie and Zafer Şenocak, eds., *Deutsche Türken/Türk Almanlar: Das Ende der Geduld/Sabrın sonu* (Reinbek bei Hamburg: Rowohlt, 1993).

74. *Intertaz* was a regular feature that grew out of an initiative organized to mark the second anniversary of the fall of the Berlin Wall. For one day, November 9, 1991, the entire *tageszeitung* was prepared by "foreign" journalists. Subsequently *intertaz* was devoted to coverage of multicultural topics; national or ethnic background was not a criterion for journalist participation.

75. In addition to the two essays translated by Judith Orban ("Tradition and Taboo") and Martin Chalmers ("War and Peace in Modernity: Reflections on a German-Turkish Future [1994]"), publication details of which can be found in the "Sources" section at the front of this book, readers can find English-language translations of some poems and literary prose

in scattered locations. Excerpts from *Mann im Unterhemd* were translated by Nancy Isenson for *Trafika* [New York and Prague] 5 (1995): 7–19. For *Descant* 83 [vol. 24, no. 4] (winter 1993–94), Judith Orban prepared translations of "Flying" (111–19), the prose piece with which *Mann im Unterhemd* opens, and two poems, "Recognitions" (120–21) and "The Blue Notebook" (122). (This is the same issue of *Descant* in which "Tradition and Taboo" appears as part of "Identity in a Foreign Place: A Conversation with Zafer Şenocak, Lakshmi Gill, and Ota Filip.") Elizabeth Oehlkers's translations of several poems can be found in two different journals. See "*Lu und andere Gedichte*/Lu and Other Poems," *Dimension2* [Austin TX] 4.2 (May 1997): 292–99; and "Between Sea and Land" and "Message in a Bottle," *Another Chicago Magazine* 32/33 (spring–summer 1997): 216–21.

76. Compare May Ayim's essay on German unification from an Afro-German perspective, "Das Jahr 1990: Heimat und Einheit aus afro-deutscher Perspektive," *Entfernte Verbindungen: Rassismus, Antisemitismus, Klassenunterdrückung*, ed. Ika Hügel et al. (Berlin: Orlanda Frauenverlag, 1993), 206–22. In the aftermath of the Rodney King beating in Los Angeles, Nahum D. Chandler offers more densely philosophical reflections on living and thinking *between*. See his essay on W. E. B. Du Bois (1868–1963), an African-American philosopher and scholar who had close personal and intellectual ties to Germany: "Between," *Assemblage: A Critical Journal of Architecture and Design Culture* 20 (1993): 26–27.

TO MY READERS IN THE UNITED STATES

1. The German original can be found in Bohrer's article, "Gibt es eine deutsche Nation?" in *Politik ohne Projekt? Nachdenken über Deutschland*, ed. Siegfried Unseld (Frankfurt a.M.: Suhrkamp, 1993), 225–35, here 225. The German nation did not exist as a unified nation-state until 1871, much later than other major European countries attained national status.

GERMANY—HOME FOR TURKS?

1. Şenocak refers here to a well-known study, published in 1975, on the Enlightenment's systemic marginalization of women, Jews, and homosexuals.

2. The full title of the book that Şenocak mentions here is *Remembering in Vain: The Klaus Barbie Trial and Crimes against Humanity*, trans. Roxanne Lapidus and Sima Godfrey (New York: Columbia University Press,

1992). Finkielkraut also wrote *Le juif imaginaire*, available in English as *The Imaginary Jew*, trans. Kevin O'Neill and David Suchoff (Lincoln: University of Nebraska Press, 1994).

WAS ADOLF HITLER AN ARAB?

1. As two of Germany's most extensively read writers of any period, Karl May (1842–1912) and Johann Wolfgang von Goethe (1749–1832) are both targets of Şenocak's biting sarcasm. That May is associated with light or "trivial" entertainment and that Goethe is the canonical German author par excellence makes little difference on this score. Karl May is best known for his travel adventure stories in "exotic" lands, especially those set in the American Wild West or the Near East. In 1892 he published one such tale titled *Durchs wilde Kurdistan* [Through wild Kurdistan]. Goethe's Orientalism in this instance concerns his *West-Östlicher Diwan* [trans. as *West-Eastern Divan*], a collection of poems published in 1819 and modeled after the poetry of Hafis, a revered Persian poet of the fourteenth century. Goethe was familiar with Hafis only on the basis of a German translation prepared by a Viennese scholar, Joseph von Hammer-Purgstall.

2. "The Old Man of the Mountain" is often used to refer to Hasan Sabbah, leader of an eleventh-century Isma'ili sect in the mountains of Syria. The word "assassins" derives from the name that Crusaders favored for members of the sect, a designation that highlights an alleged proclivity to violence, murder, and hashish consumption. For a recent account of the sect's history and the legends surrounding it, see Farhad Daftary, *The Assassin Legends: Myths of the Isma'ilis* (London: Tauris, 1994). Today German media often invoke the Assassins as an ostensible precursor to modern terrorists. Saladin is the common German spelling for Salah ah-Din (1138–93), sultan of Egypt and Syria, a historical figure who for centuries has appeared as an Oriental stereotype in popular German culture. As Aijaz Ahmad tells us, Salah ah-Din was "much reviled by later centuries throughout Christendom, because he was in fact a commander of the Arab-Islamic forces that were ranged against the Crusading Christians" (*In Theory*, 189).

"ORIENT" AND "OCCIDENT"

1. Şenocak's source for the saying (*hadîth*) that he attributes to Muhammad is itself a Turkish translation from Arabic. See no. 2687 in Mehmet

Sofuoğlu, ed., *Sahihi Muslim*, vol. 8 (Istanbul: Irfan Yayınevi, 1972), 175. My English translation is based on Şenocak's German rendition of the *hadîth*. Scholarship indicates that the full text of this saying belongs to the genre of hadîth qudsî (divine saying). In this tradition the Prophet recounts the words of God; the "I" in the quotation thus refers to God, not to Muhammad.

The Goethe quotation derives from a letter dated September 25, 1820. See no. 186 in *Goethes Werke*, edited as commissioned by the Grand Duchess Sophie of Saxony, IV. Abt., vol. 33 (Weimar: Hermann Böhlaus Nachfolger, 1905), 255. The full text of the passage concerns Goethe's perception that women are better suited to understanding than men.

2. While the first paragraph is an obvious reference to Salman Rushdie's *The Satanic Verses* (1988), readers may be less familiar with the book described in the second paragraph. The book in question is Betty Mahmoody's *Not without My Daughter* (1987), the German translation of which (*Nicht ohne meine Tochter*, 1988) had a much higher publication run than the original publication in the United States. In 1990 Mahmoody's story of international parental kidnapping was made into a film starring Sally Field and Alfred Molina. For these and other details concerning the German reception of Mahmoody's account, see Anne-Kathrin Reulecke, " 'Die Befreiung aus dem Serail': Betty Mahmoodys Roman *Nicht ohne meine Tochter*," in *Das Schwert des "Experten": Peter Scholl-Latours verzerrtes Araber- und Islambild*, ed. Verena Klemm and Karin Hörner (Heidelberg: Palmyra, 1993), 229–50.

3. As a concept developed in the Enlightenment philosophy of Immanuel Kant (1724–1804), *Mündigkeit* does not lend itself happily to English translation. "Reasoned majority" conveys the linkage that Kant posited between an individual's capacity to use reason critically and the ability to attain personal maturity and political autonomy because of it. In this context "majority" is not a quantitative term but a philosophical one.

4. The 1950s in Turkey saw the rise of poetry and fiction depicting the misery of peasant life. The genre of the "village novel" is most famously associated with Yaşar Kemal, the world-renowned author of *İnce Memed* (1955), available in Edouard Roditi's English translation as *Memed, My Hawk* (London: Collins Harvill, 1990). In October 1997 Kemal was awarded the prestigious Peace Prize of the German Book Trade, the same prize that would be awarded to Martin Walser one year later. The award ceremony for Kemal also sparked a major public controversy after the

German writer Günter Grass used the occasion of his *laudatio* for Kemal to criticize the German government for denying citizenship to its resident Turks and Kurds and for supplying weapons to the Turkish government in its "war of destruction" against the Kurds. The full text of Grass's speech and other relevant documentation of the German controversy can be found in Manfred Bissinger and Daniela Hermes, eds., *Zeit, sich einzumischen* (Göttingen: Steidl, 1998).

5. Founder of the Mevlevi Order (known in the West as the "whirling dervishes"), Mevlana Jalal al-Din Rumi (1207–73) was an Islamic mystic whose influence on Persian and Turkish cultures has been considerable.

6. Şenocak's perspective here is comparative rather than absolute. For insights into a gripping novel at the crossroads of France, Algeria, and Germany, see the third chapter of Dominick LaCapra's *History and Memory after Auschwitz* (Ithaca NY: Cornell University Press, 1998): "Reading Camus's *The Fall* after Auschwitz and with Algeria" (73–94). In a related vein, see Hélène Cixous's haunting, lyrical autobiographical essay, "My Algeriance: In Other Words, to Depart Not to Arrive from Algeria," trans. Eric Prenowitz, *TriQuarterly* 100 (fall 1997): 259–79.

THE ISLAND

1. The "old man" here refers to Gerhart Hauptmann (1862–1946), one of Germany's most celebrated authors of naturalist prose and drama. Winner of the Nobel Prize for literature in 1912, he is buried on the Baltic Sea island of Hiddensee. Between 1949 and the national unification of 1990, Hiddensee belonged to the German Democratic Republic. This travelogue's occasional references to the communist past conjure a period of German life on Hiddensee after Hauptmann's death. Additionally, both before and after the author's death, his sympathetic literary depiction of working-class misery was embraced by the cultural politics of German socialists and communists. Although "The Island" of this travelogue refers to Hiddensee, readers may also be interested to know that it lies very close to the better-known island of Rügen. A Berlin publishing house has advertised a new collection of essays as delineating "the mythical topography" of Rügen as a *lieu de mémoire* for the German nation. See Roswitha Schieb and Gregor Wedekind, eds., *Rügen: Deutschlands mythische Insel* (Berlin: Berlin Vlg., 1999).

2. *Heimatliteratur* designates German literature that conservatively cele-

brates rural life and regional loyalties to the land. The heyday of this literature, which takes an impassioned stand against modernity, was in the very early years of the twentieth century. Colonialist and fascist writers could easily appropriate its hallmarks.

3. This is an allusion to institutionalized Communist Party leadership.

WHAT DOES THE FOREST DYING HAVE TO DO WITH MULTICULTURALISM?

1. The forest dying (*Waldsterben*) has been a much publicized environmental concern in the Federal Republic. The German forest also carries considerable symbolic weight in Germanic mythologies and some (generally conservative) political movements of the nineteenth and twentieth centuries.

2. In some circles Heiner Geißler is credited with first using the term "multicultural" to describe what the Federal Republic should strive to be. Trained in philosophy and law, the CDU politician served his party as secretary general for twelve years. Favoring a liberalization of foreigners' rights as early as ten years ago, he published his own book on Germany as a multicultural society, *Zugluft* (Munich: Bertelsmann, 1990). The phrase "constitutional patriotism" (*Verfassungspatriotismus*) stems from the political social philosophy of Jürgen Habermas, the foremost representative of the second generation of the Frankfurt School of Critical Theory, known primarily for his studies on communicative rationality, intersubjectivity, and the public sphere. In public debates of the 1980s Habermas took a strong stance in favor of the only kind of patriotism he deems viable for Germany. This would rest on loyalty to the rational democratic values of a national constitution, not to an exclusionary ethnic model of German identity.

3. The German term translated here as "religious dogmatists" is *Integralisten*. This should not be confused with liberal precepts of integration.

4. Max Horkheimer and Theodor W. Adorno, *Dialectic of Enlightenment*, trans. John Cumming (New York: Herder and Herder, 1972), 181–82. Horkheimer and Adorno cite Sigmund Freud's essay "The Uncanny" at this moment in their essay.

TRADITION AND TABOO

1. Minor emendations in the translation have been made by the editor.

THE POET AND THE DESERTERS

1. Thomas Aquinas (c. 1224–74) is renowned above all other Christian theologians, ethicists, and philosophers of the Middle Ages. Şenocak refers to various manifestations of medieval poetry and courtly love in a subsequent sentence.

2. This German Jewish philosopher (1885–1977) is better known for his unorthodox contributions to Marxist theories of aesthetics and politics, especially his *Geist der Utopie* [The spirit of utopia, 1919/1923] and *Das Prinzip Hoffnung* [*The Principle of Hope*, 1959]. His book on Avicenna was first published in 1952.

3. The essay cites Balić's article "Die Moslems in Bosnien," in *Renaissance des Islams: Wege zur Begegnung oder zur Konfrontation?*, ed. Michael Fitzgerald et al. (Graz: Styria, 1980), 97–126.

4. This journal began publication in 1970 in Sarajevo. Vol. 21 was published in 1990. I have not been able to ascertain whether the journal is still being published today.

5. These two bracketed deletions involve an extended quotation from Rushdie's *The Satanic Verses*. The passage cited from the novel entails one character's description of "the proposed metamorphosis of London into a tropical city" (354–55).

6. The bracketed deletion is a quotation from Rushdie's essay "In Good Faith," in *Imaginary Homelands: Essays and Criticism, 1981–1991* (London: Granta, 1991), 393–414, here 394: "Throughout human history, the apostles of purity, those who have claimed to possess a total explanation, have wrought havoc among mere mixed-up human beings. Like many millions of people, I am a bastard child of history. Perhaps we all are, black and brown and white, leaking into one another, as a character of mine once said, *like flavours when you cook*." Şenocak's subsequent reference to "the bastardization of European literature" echoes Rushdie's description of himself as "a bastard child of history." Readers unfamiliar with Rushdie's essays may be interested to know that *Imaginary Homelands* contains several short essays on well-known German writers such as Günter Grass, Heinrich Böll, Siegfried Lenz, Peter Schneider, and the Austrian Christoph Ransmayr.

7. The reference is to Ram A. Mall, "Die orthafte Ortlosigkeit der Hermeneutik: Zur Kritik der reduktiven Hermeneutik," *Widerspruch: Münchner Zeitschrift für Philosophie* 15 (1988): 38–49, here 43.

THE CONCEPT OF CULTURE AND ITS DISCONTENTS

1. The verb *verklären* can mean to mystify, to render transcendent, or—as a pun on *erklären* (to explain)—to mangle explanation.

GERMANY IS MORE A LANGUAGE THAN A LAND

1. This English translation has been prepared on the basis of Mine Dal and Karin Yeşilada's unpublished translation of the Turkish original into German. The Turkish interview was published in Istanbul as "Almanya Bir Ülke Olmaktan Çok Bir Dildir," *Kitaplık* [Bookcase] 12 (October– December 1994): 24.

2. Franz Kafka (1883–1924), Ingeborg Bachmann (1926–73), Rainer Maria Rilke (1875–1926), and Georg Trakl (1887–1914) are all well known authors of modern literature in German.

3. The interviewer alludes here to the publication of "Tradition and Taboo" in the Parisian journal *Anka* 18/19 (May 1993): 233–35, in a special issue in the series *Les belles Étrangères*.

4. Gökhan refers here to a French translation of an essay originally published in German in Şenocak's 1992 *Atlas* ("Wann ist der Fremde zu Hause?" 64–75). The French version appeared in *Hommes et migrations* 1151–52 (February–March 1992): 50–54.

5. In very different contexts the writings of Franz Kafka and Albert Camus (1913–60) have often been interpreted in terms of existential alienation and unnerving estrangement. One of Camus's more famous works even bears the title *The Stranger* (*L'Étranger*, 1942). The French Algerian author, who felt partial affinities with Arabs oppressed by French colonialism, received the Nobel Prize for literature in 1957. As for Kafka, a Jewish artist of German literature written in the German, Czech, Yiddish, and Hebrew milieu of Prague, the many dimensions of Camus's estrangement defy glib categorization.

6. Necatigil (1916–79) was a major Turkish poet. Two of his poems about houses can be found in English translation as "Eternal House," trans. Feyyaz Kayacan, and "The War of the Houses," trans. Nermin Menemencioğlu, in Talat Sait Halman, ed., *Contemporary Turkish Literature: Fiction and Poetry* (London: Associated University Presses, 1982), 366 and 369–70, respectively. In addition to writing poetry, Necatigil also translated works by European authors into Turkish, the postwar German author Wolfgang Borchert among them.

7. Yunus Emre was a fourteenth-century Anatolian mystic whose poetry has been of central importance for both Bektaşi Sufism and Turkish literature generally. Kaygusuz Abdal, Pir Sultan Abdal, and Karacaoğlan were folk poets from the fifteenth, sixteenth, and seventeenth centuries, respectively. Şencoak's translations of poems by Pir Sultan Abdal can be found in *Sirene* 1 (1988): 58–83. His bilingual edition of Yunus Emre's poetry was published as *Das Kummerrad/Dertli Dolap* (Frankfurt a. M.: Dağyeli, 1986).

MAY ONE COMPARE TURKS AND JEWS, MR. ŞENOCAK?

1. In postwar Germany *Schicksalsgemeinschaft* has been a common diplomatic euphemism for the historical relationship between Germans and Jews in the twentieth century, especially that marked by the Nazis' attempt to annihilate European Jewry.

2. The reference to packaged buildings is to Christo and Jeanne-Claude's *Wrapped Reichstag* project, one of the more spectacular and festive events of 1995, which was generally a year of many historical commemorations. Unlike the commemorative events of 1985, which marked the fortieth anniversary of everything associated with 1945, the fiftieth anniversary was celebrated in the wake of unification. For additional commentary, see Lutz P. Koepnick, "Rethinking the Spectacle: History, Visual Culture, and German Unification," in *Wendezeiten, Zeitenwenden: Positionsbestimmungen zur deutschsprachigen Literatur, 1945–1995*, ed. Robert Weninger and Brigitte Rossbacher (Tübingen: Stauffenburg, 1997), 151–70.

3. The author alludes here to Gershom Scholem, the great twentieth-century German and Israeli scholar of Jewish mysticism. Although his own relationship to Zionism was conflicted, Scholem famously contended that the much touted "German-Jewish dialogue" had never existed. See his essays, *On Jews and Judaism in Crisis* (New York: Schocken, 1976).

4. The editorial introduction discusses Ignatz Bubis, who headed the Central Council of Jews in Germany from 1992 until his death in 1999, in conjunction with the Walser Debate of 1998. Michel Friedman, long active in shaping the cultural policies of the Jewish community in Frankfurt am Main, held the second highest administrative position in the Central Council.

5. This is a reference to a collection of essays edited by Şenocak, *Der ge-*

brochene Blick nach Westen: Positionen und Perspektiven türkischer Kultur (Berlin: Babel, 1994).

6. Tansu Çiller was prime minister of the Republic of Turkey in 1995.

THOUGHTS ON MAY 8, 1995

1. The "godless republic" is an allusion to the aggressively secular platform on which the Western-oriented Republic of Turkey was founded in 1923. With "these godless others" the author means the Soviet Union and the kind of atheism mandated by the communist state.

2. The notion of Germany as a *Kulturnation* dates back to the eighteenth century, long before any political entity known as the German nation was established in 1871. The various relationships between Germany as a *Kulturnation* and any actual German state formation continue to be hotly debated.

3. In this context *Wiedergutmachung* means both something concrete and something intangible. On the one hand, Germany signed a formal agreement with the state of Israel in 1952 to regulate financial reparations to be made by the Federal Republic for property losses suffered by Jewish victims of the Nazi regime. (This agreement was very controversial among surviving Jews and especially in Israel, where Menachem Begin led an aggressive campaign against it.) On the other hand, *Wiedergutmachung* translates literally as "[the] making good again." In the figurative sense the word thus applies to intersubjective efforts by Germans to make amends for human losses that can never be set right again. Both senses of the word influence more recent debates (1990s) about reparations for slave labor that Jewish, Sinti, Roma, and Polish victims of the Nazis were forced to perform for the benefit of some German industries.

BETWEEN ORIENT AND OCCIDENT

1. The 1994 volume of Şenocak's essays, *War Hitler Araber?*, opens with a piece titled "Ingenieure des Glaubens" [Engineers of faith]. The author coined this term in critical reference to both religious fundamentalists and European Orientalists, two groups that have, in his view, used different means to perpetuate the same myth of Islam as incapable of and impervious to historical and social change. Noting the high number of engineers involved in fundamentalist movements in countries such as Algeria, Egypt, Iran, and Turkey, he remarks on the "widespread postcolonial misprision" that technological advances are completely divorced from culture and tradition (17).

2. The German words *integristisch* and *Integralisten* have to do with religious dogmatism, not "integration" in its liberal sense. The "last, perfect revelation" refers to a central theological tenet of Islam, which holds that divine truth as revealed in Islam supersedes that of its predecessor religions, notably Judaism and Christianity.

3. Pir Sultan Abdal is better known as a Turkish folk poet of the sixteenth century who was put to death for allegedly conspiring with enemies of the Ottoman Empire. The twelfth-century Persian poet and mathematician Omar Khayyam is known in the West largely through a nineteenth-century translation of his poetry, *The Rubayyat of Omar Khayyam*. The Mansur at issue here is Husayn ibn Mansur al-Hallaj, an intensely controversial and tormented Islamic mystic whose life spanned the late ninth and early tenth centuries. He was subjected to long imprisonment and death by torture, in part for having declared, "I am the Truth." See Annemarie Schimmel, *Mystical Dimensions of Islam* (Chapel Hill: University of North Carolina Press, 1975), 62–77.

4. This pun relies on the "hermeneutic circle" of understanding and interpretation. As developed over the last three centuries by German philosophers such as Friedrich Schleiermacher, Wilhelm Dilthey, Martin Heidegger, and Hans-Georg Gadamer, the term articulates relationships between a whole and its parts, between past and present, and between subject and object.

5. Here the author criticizes what he perceives as the tendency in Islamic cultures today to promote a reductive understanding of Enlightenment.

6. The author mentions Paul Feyerabend and Ivan Illich as examples of Western scholars whose critiques of rationalism, science, education, and society figure on the Turkish intellectual landscape as well. See Paul Feyerabend, *Farewell to Reason* (London: Verso, 1987), and *Against Method: Outline of an Anarchistic Theory of Knowledge* (London: NLB, 1975; New York: Verso, 1993); Ivan Illich, *In the Mirror of the Past: Lectures and Addresses, 1978–1990* (New York: Boyars, 1992).

BEYOND THE LANGUAGE OF THE LAND

1. The bureaucratic designation stems from the East German state security apparatus (Stasi), which involved many GDR citizens in varying levels of clandestine surveillance on neighbors, relatives, friends, and colleagues. Once Stasi files became available for public scrutiny in the wake of unification, news of those who had served as IM spread like wildfire,

destroying many relationships and igniting moralistic recriminations along with political debate.

PAUL CELAN

1. This essay is a modified version of remarks presented at a Parisian conference on Paul Celan in November 1995. The German text of that presentation can be found in *Sirene* 9.15/16 (March 1996): 166–70. In *Sirene* the text of Şenocak's conference presentation on Celan directly precedes "Jenseits der Landessprache" ["Beyond the Language of the Land"]. The sequence of these two essays is reversed in this *Atlas*.

2. This is not a direct quotation from Celan, but rather Şenocak's formulation of a question that he ascribes to Celan's poetry. There has been no consensus on an adequate translation of Ingeborg Bachmann's original declarative formulation, "Die Wahrheit ist dem Menschen zumutbar," which was the title of her acceptance speech upon receiving the Radio Play Prize of the War Blind in 1959. In Patricia A. Herminghouse, ed., *Ingeborg Bachmann and Christa Wolf: Selected Prose and Drama* (New York: Continuum, 1998), 101–12, one finds Jan van Heurck's translation of "The Truth You Can Expect," the essay that Wolf wrote about Bachmann in 1966. An editorial note by Herminghouse indicates that *die zumutbare Wahrheit* is "better translated as 'The Truth One Can Face'" (101). The translation modified for the Şenocak essay allows more readily for the kind of linkage posited by Şenocak between Bachmann and Celan. Other forms of personal and intellectual influence by Celan on Bachmann are well established.

3. The Kabbalah includes all elements of Jewish mysticism. Sufism refers to Islamic mysticism. (The early Republic of Turkey took a strong stance against the Sufis, decreeing their mystical orders illegal in 1928.)

4. Because of the echo that exists in German between *Niemandsland* and "*Niemandsrose*," the translator has taken the liberty of deviating from Michael Hamburger's translation of the latter as "no one's rose." See *Poems of Paul Celan*, trans. Michael Hamburger (New York: Persea, 1988), 175. Found in the poem "Psalm," *Niemandsrose* is Celan's coinage and the title of a book of his poetry that was published in 1963. Hamburger's translation ("the no one's rose") does more justice to the mystical dimensions of Celan's "Psalm." Although mysticism also plays a role in Şenocak's use of *Niemandsrose*, his poetic reflections on "place" and "land" make "no-man's-rose" a more apt counterpart to "no-man's-land."

THE ONE AND THE OTHER CHILD

1. A slightly modified version of this otherwise unpublished piece, originally written in 1996, appears on pages 98–99 of the author's novel
Gefährliche Verwandtschaft, which was published in 1998.

TERRITORIES

1. The author relies on a word play here that does not lend itself to punning
in English. Both *Stammbaum* and *Stammtisch* are compound nouns, and
in both instances the first part of the word is *Stamm*, which can mean
trunk, tribe, or stem. *Baum* means tree, and *Tisch* means table. The
compound *Stammbaum* refers to a genealogical tree, while *Stammtisch*
refers to a table reserved for regular customers in a restaurant or bar. This
practice tends to be associated with a predilection for familiarity and
exclusion.

WHICH MYTH WRITES ME?

1. Peter Weiss (1916–82) authored two especially notable plays that gar-
nered him an international reputation for boldly mixing theater and politics. *Die Verfolgung und Ermordung Jean Paul Marats, dargestellt durch
die Schauspielgruppe des Hospizes zu Charenton unter Anleitung des Herrn
de Sade* (1964) is more commonly called *Marat/Sade*. When the Auschwitz trials in Frankfurt am Main ended in 1965, the play that Weiss had
written based on the court proceedings (*Die Ermittlung*; English: *The
Investigation*) opened simultaneously on many stages throughout Germany. Weiss's autobiographical writings revolved around exile and other
forms of estrangement. Although he had been raised as a German Protestant in Germany, his family's Czech citizenship and his father's Jewish
background gave them pressing reasons to flee the Nazi regime. Weiss
spent most of his exile in Stockholm and much of his life in contempla-
tion of his personal relationship to Auschwitz, where he was never in-
terned. See his essay "My Place," trans. Christopher Middleton, in *German Writing Today*, ed. Christopher Middleton (Harmondsworth:
Penguin, 1967), 20–28.

2. The revolutionizing generational experience meant here concerns Atatürk's sweeping and dramatic reforms of the 1920s and 1930s.

3. Unconventional philosophical reflections by Walter Benjamin (1892–
1940), who killed himself while trying, unsuccessfully, to escape Nazi-
occupied Europe, have been enormously influential in many countries.
For insights into the varied German Jewish relations that shaped the lives

of authors that Şenocak mentions here and elsewhere, see the relevant entries in Sander L. Gilman and Jack Zipes, eds., *Yale Companion to Jewish Writing and Thought in German Culture, 1096–1996* (New Haven CT: Yale University Press, 1997).

WAR AND PEACE IN MODERNITY

1. Martin Chalmers translated a version of this essay that was written in 1994. His translation appeared in *Cultural Studies* 10.2 (May 1996): 255–69 with a critical introduction by Kevin Robins (255–58). Additional sections written in 1998 have been translated by Leslie A. Adelson, and minor emendations in the Chalmers translation have been made in keeping with the editorial preferences guiding the larger translation project of this book. Although the German version of the essay in its present form has not been previously published, an earlier version did appear as "Krieg und Frieden in Deutschland: Gedanken über die deutsch-türkische Zukunft," in *Anderssein, ein Menschenrecht: Über die Vereinbarkeit universaler Normen mit kultureller und ethnischer Vielfalt*, ed. Hilmar Hoffmann and Dieter Kramer (Weinheim: Beltz Athenäum, 1995), 115–23. That version does not correspond to the Chalmers translation either.

2. Joseph Rudyard Kipling (1865–1936) was the 1907 recipient of the Nobel Prize for literature. A British colonial author of many tales and poems about "the East" and India especially, Kipling also penned *The Jungle Book*, familiar to many American readers today in its incarnation as a Walt Disney film. The phrase cited above stems from the verse with which Kipling's *Ballad of East and West* (New York: Alex Grosset, 1904) both opens and closes: "Oh, East is East, and West is West, / and never the two shall meet, / Till Earth and Sky stand presently at God's great Judgment Seat. / But there is neither East nor West, Border, nor Breed, nor Birth, / When two strong men stand face to face, tho' they come from the ends of the earth" (n.p.). Şenocak's bitterly ironic confirmation of Kipling's famous dictum goes to the core of the former's concerns about political conflicts falsely construed as cultural difference.

3. Remo Guidieri, "Les Sociétés primitives aujourd'hui," in *Philosopher: Les interrogations contemporaines*, ed. Christian Delacampagne and Robert Maggiori (Paris: Fayard, 1980), 60.

4. The reference is to "Anschwellender Bocksgesang," *Spiegel* 47.6 (February 8, 1993): 202–7. (See editorial introduction and n. 62 for additional

information.) Chalmers's translation of "die Verhöhnung des Eros, die Verhöhnung des Soldaten" as "the ridiculing of heroes, the ridiculing of soldiers" (*Cultural Studies* 10.2 [1996]: 262) has been slightly modified in keeping with the editor's understanding of Strauss's use of language.

5. Here the author means the Ayatollah Khomeini.

6. See n. 62 to the editor's introduction for full bibliographical references. For the German original of the paragraphs cited, see *Die selbstbewusste Nation*, 21–22.

7. Here and in two subsequent locations, brackets indicate text that the author deleted in revising his essay for 1998. These deleted sections are included in the Chalmers translation published in 1996.

8. Şenocak alludes here to Walter Benjamin's famous essay of 1935 "Das Kunstwerk im Zeitalter seiner technischen Reproduzierbarkeit" ["The Work of Art in the Age of Mechanical Reproduction"].

9. Religion is a regular subject in German public schools. Martin Luther (1483–1546), who translated the New Testament into German, was excommunicated from the Roman Catholic Church in 1520 for his stridently prominent role in the Protestant Reformation and his bold defiance of papal authority. He hated Turks as much as he despised the pope. See Martin Luther, *Table Talk*, trans. William Hazlitt (London: Fount, 1995), where one reads, "Antichrist is the pope and the Turk together; a beast full of life must have a body and soul; the spirit or soul of Antichrist, is the pope, his flesh or body the Turk" (214). (Bernard Lewis cites a very slightly modified version of this passage in *Islam and the West* [73].) Şenocak himself cites a 1566 edition of *Martin Luthers Tischreden*, as collected and printed by Johannes Aurifaber in Eisleben. Compare entry no. 904, in *D. Martin Luthers Werke, kritische Gesamtausgabe*, vol. 1, *Tischreden*, ed. Karl Drescher (Weimar: Hermann Böhlaus Nachfolger, 1912), 449. Drescher notes that this entry corresponds to no. 2706 in Aurifaber. The content of the Aurifaber entry cited by Şenocak and that cited by Drescher is virtually the same, though the phrasing is not identical. The translation here follows the citation in Şenocak's essay.

10. In the field of popular journalism in Germany, Peter Scholl-Latour stands out for his notoriously antagonistic but widely published and widely read commentaries on Arabs, Turks, and Islam. During the Persian Gulf War in January 1991, a major television station (zdf) broadcast a special four-part series by Scholl-Latour on Islam, with barbed emphasis on the inexorable dangers that he associates with Muslims and

their religion. The television series bore the same title as the book designed to accompany it, *Das Schwert des Islam* (Munich: Heyne, 1990), which quickly became a bestseller. Scholl-Latour is not without his German critics. Several of them collaborated on an anthology debunking his claims to expertise on the subject of Islam and taking him sharply to task for the xenophobic panic and prejudice that he tends to fuel. See Verena Klemm and Karin Hörner, eds., *Das Schwert des "Experten": Peter Scholl-Latours verzerrtes Araber- und Islambild* (Heidelberg: Palmyra, 1993). See Said, *Covering Islam* (1981, 1997), for his analysis of comparable problems that arise when "the media and the experts" join forces to demonize Islam.

11. The Luther sermon at issue is Martin Luther's *Heerpredigt: Wider den Türcken* [Troops Sermon: Against the Turk] (Augsburg: Hainrich Stainer, 1542), in which the Reformation theologian explained why, in his view, Christians should wage war against the Turks of the Ottoman Empire for secular rather than religious reasons and, furthermore, how they should behave if captured. For the English translation of an earlier treatise on related themes, see Luther's "On War against the Turk, 1529," trans. Charles M. Jacobs, rev. Robert C. Schultz, in *Luther's Works*, ed. Jaroslav Pelikan and Helmut T. Lehmann, vol. 46, ed. Robert C. Schultz (Philadelphia: Fortress, 1967), 161–205.

12. Walser's comments appeared in an article (on national identity and liberal German aversions to it) titled "Deutsche Sorgen," *Spiegel* 47.26 (June 28, 1993): 40–47. The reference to billeting appears on p. 45.

13. Augstein's remarks can be found in "Heilmittel 'Doppelbürger'?" *Spiegel* 47.23 (June 7, 1993): 18. Chalmers provides a note explaining that Prince Eugene (1663–1736) was the Austrian imperial general renowned for his military victories against the armies of the Ottoman Empire, including the capture of Belgrade. The cover story for this *Spiegel* issue was "Die deutschen Türken: Opfer des Fremdenhasses," prompted by the deadly attack on Turks in Solingen on May 29.

14. Historical relationships between Turks and Arabs have been complicated, as evidenced in the twentieth century by Atatürk's desire to eliminate Arabic and Persian influences on modern Turkish language and culture. In the context of this essay, the reference to Arabs in France and Turks in Germany is to significant "non-European" minority populations in these two European countries.

15. This translation diverges from Martin Chalmers's preference for "regulated and mastered" at the conclusion of this sentence (*Cultural Studies* 10.2 [May 1996]: 268). The German original reads, "Für denjenigen aber, der in den Metropolen Europas zu Hause ist, die alle torn cities sind, ist Zerrissenheit ein Zustand, von dessen Regelung und Meisterung unser aller Zukunft abhängt" (author's ms.).

Other Books by Zafer Şenocak

IN GERMAN

Elektrisches Blau: Gedichte. Munich: Ströme, 1983.

Verkauf der Morgenstimmungen am Markt: Gedichte. Munich: Literazette, 1983.

Flammentropfen: Gedichte. Frankfurt a. M.: Dağyeli, 1985.

Ritual der Jugend: Gedichte. Frankfurt a. M.: Dağyeli, 1987.

Das senkrechte Meer: Gedichte. Berlin: Babel, 1991.

Ed. with Deniz Göktürk. *Jedem Wort gehört ein Himmel: Türkei literarisch.* Berlin: Babel, 1991.

Atlas des tropischen Deutschland: Essays. Berlin: Babel, 1992.

Ed. with Claus Leggewie. *Deutsche Türken/Türk Almanlar: Das Ende der Geduld/Sabrın Sonu.* Reinbek bei Hamburg: Rowohlt, 1993.

War Hitler Araber? IrreFührungen an den Rand Europas, Essays. Berlin: Babel, 1994.

Fernwehanstalten: Gedichte. Berlin: Babel, 1994.

Ed. *Der gebrochene Blick nach Westen: Positionen und Perspektiven türkischer Kultur.* Berlin: Babel, 1994.

Der Mann im Unterhemd. Berlin: Babel, 1995.

Die Prärie. Berlin: Rotbuch, 1997.

Gefährliche Verwandtschaft: Roman. Berlin: Babel, 1998.

Der Erottomane: Ein Findelbuch. Munich, Babel, 1999.

IN TRANSLATION

Gençlik Ayinleri. Trans. Yüksel Özoğuz. Istanbul: Yapı Kredi Yayınları, 1994.

Hitler Arap Mıydı? Denemeler. Trans. Mustafa Tüzel. Istanbul: Kabalcı Yayınevi, 1997.

Atletli Adam. Trans. Mustafa Tüzel and Vedat Çorlu. Istanbul: Kabalcı Yayınevi, 1997.

La Mer verticale. Trans. Timour Muhidine. Paris: L'Esprit des Péninsules, 1999.

Other Books by Zafer Şenocak

TRANSLATIONS BY THE AUTHOR

Fethi Savaşçi. *München im Frühlingsregen: Erzählungen*. Frankfurt a.M.: Dağyeli, 1986.

Yunus Emre. *Das Kummerrad/Dertli Dolap: Gedichte*. Frankfurt a.M.: Dağyeli, 1986.

Aras Ören. *Eine verspätete Abrechnung oder Der Aufstieg der Gündoğdus: Roman*. Trans. with Eva Hund. Frankfurt a.M.: Dağyeli, 1988.

———. *Uhrmacher der Einsamkeit: Gedichte*. Trans. with Eva Hund. Berlin: Mariannenpresse, 1993.

For periodically updated bibliography and commentary on the author, readers are referred to Karin Yeşilada, "Zafer Şenocak," in *Kritisches Lexikon zur deutschsprachigen Gegenwartsliteratur*, ed. Heinz Ludwig Arnold (Munich: edition text + kritik, n.d.), a looseleaf reference work on contemporary authors of German literature.

Index

In the *Texts and Contexts* series

Affective Genealogies
*Psychoanalysis, Postmodernism, and the
"Jewish Question" after Auschwitz*
By Elizabeth J. Bellamy

Sojourners
The Return of German Jews and the Question of Identity
By John Borneman and Jeffrey M. Peck

Serenity in Crisis
A Preface to Paul de Man, 1939–1960
By Ortwin de Graef

Titanic Light
Paul de Man's Post-Romanticism, 1960–1969
By Ortwin de Graef

The Future of a Negation
Reflections on the Question of Genocide
By Alain Finkielkraut
Translated by Mary Byrd Kelly

The Imaginary Jew
By Alain Finkielkraut
Translated by Kevin O'Neill and David Suchoff

The Wisdom of Love
By Alain Finkielkraut
Translated by Kevin O'Neill and David Suchoff

The House of Joshua
Meditations on Family and Place
By Mindy Thompson Fullilove

Inscribing the Other
By Sander L. Gilman

**Antisemitism, Misogyny, and the Logic of
Cultural Difference**
Cesare Lombroso and Matilde Serao
By Nancy A. Harrowitz

Opera
Desire, Disease, Death
By Linda Hutcheon and Michael Hutcheon

Man of Ashes
By Salomon Isacovici and Juan Manuel Rodríguez
Translated by Dick Gerdes

Between Redemption and Doom
The Strains of German-Jewish Modernism
By Noah Isenberg

Poetic Process
By W. G. Kudszus

Keepers of the Motherland
German Texts by Jewish Women Writers
By Dagmar C. G. Lorenz

Madness and Art
The Life and Works of Adolf Wölfli
By Walter Morgenthaler
Translated and with an introduction by
Aaron H. Esman
in collaboration with Elka Spoerri

Organic Memory
*History and the Body in the Late Nineteenth
and Early Twentieth Centuries*
By Laura Otis

Crack Wars
Literature, Addiction, Mania
By Avital Ronell

Finitude's Score
Essays for the End of the Millennium
By Avital Ronell

Herbarium/Verbarium
The Discourse of Flowers
By Claudette Sartiliot

Atlas of a Tropical Germany
Essays on Politics and Culture, 1990–1998
By Zafer Şenocak
Translated and with an introduction by Leslie A. Adelson

Budapest Diary
In Search of the Motherbook
By Susan Rubin Suleiman

Rahel Levin Varnhagen
The Life and Work of a German Jewish Intellectual
By Heidi Thomann Tewarson

The Jews and Germany
From the "Judeo-German Symbiosis"
to the Memory of Auschwitz
By Enzo Traverso
Translated by Daniel Weissbort

Richard Wagner and the Anti-Semitic Imagination
By Marc A. Weiner

Undertones of Insurrection
Music, Politics, and the Social Sphere
in the Modern German Narrative
By Marc A. Weiner

The Mirror and the Word
Modernism, Literary Theory, and Georg Trakl
By Eric B. Williams